ENDORSEMENTS

Jesus told us *"Seek first the kingdom of heaven, and all else will be added"* to us. Dr. Trimm's book provides a recipe for seeking that will surely yield eternal results. Her writing is clear, her focus is sure, and her aim is true. Read this, and be magnified.

LAURIE BETH JONES
Author, *Jesus, CEO*; *The Path*;
Jesus, Life Coach; *The Four Elements of Success*

The Prosperous Soul is more than a book. It is a master's degree in how to obtain the right mindset to thrive in a world of uncertainty. Dr. Trimm takes a focused inch-wide approach to writing about prosperity and then drills down a mile deep in providing wisdom, research, and easily adaptable, actionable steps that anyone can use. I kept turning page after page, wanting more and more, and got it. I am going to tell everyone that I know to get this book. In fact, I want my children to read it and live it. *The Prosperous Soul* will teach you how to stop chasing money and make money chase you.

SIMON T. BAILEY
Author of *Shift Your Brilliance*, Leadership Imagineer,
and founder of Brilliance Institute

The PROSPEROUS *Soul*

DESTINY IMAGE BOOKS BY DR. CINDY TRIMM

The 40 Day Soul Fast

40 Days to Discovering the Real You

Reclaim Your Soul

40 Days to Reclaiming Your Soul

The Prosperous Soul

40 Days to a Prosperous Soul

Push

Prevail

Heal Your Soul, Heal Our World
(Coming Soon!)

The PROSPEROUS Soul

Your Journey to a Richer Life

CINDY TRIMM

Manuscript prepared by Rick and Melissa Killian, Killian Creative, Boulder, Colorado. www.killiancreative.com.

Cover design by River Publishing

DESTINY IMAGE® PUBLISHERS, INC.
P.O. Box 310, Shippensburg, PA 17257-0310
"Promoting Inspired Lives."

This book and all other Destiny Image and Destiny Image Fiction books are available at Christian bookstores and distributors worldwide.
For more information on foreign distributors, call 717-532-3040.
Reach us on the Internet: www.destinyimage.com.

ISBN 13 HC: 978-0-7684-1299-4
ISBN 13 TP: 978-0-7684-0518-7
ISBN 13 Ebook: 978-0-7684-0519-4

For Worldwide Distribution, Printed in the U.S.A.
1 2 3 4 5 6 7 8 / 19 18 17 16 15

DEDICATION AND ACKNOWLEDGMENTS

To all who desire to see God's abundance manifested in the lives of His children—His wholeness, His peace, His best will for humankind—and to all who continue daily in hot pursuit of His Kingdom and His righteousness. May all you set your hands and hearts to prosper!

To Rick & Melissa Killian, thank you for setting your editorial hand to this manuscript—your brilliant perspective, research, and input helped to shape this work into what it is today.

To my publishers, thank you once again for believing in the relevance of my message and providing the resources to get this message out.

To Gail Lightbourne, Natasha Cozart, and single mothers everywhere, may your lives be ever richer!

Beloved, I pray that you may prosper in all things and be in health, just as your soul prospers.[1]

—Jesus

CONTENTS

Those who knew Anne best felt without realizing it that her greatest attraction was the aura of possibility surrounding her...the power of future development that was in her. She seemed to walk in an atmosphere of things about to happen.

—Lucy Maud Montgomery,
Anne of Avonlea

FOREWORD

There is a profound old saying that states, "Success in life does not depend on where you come from, it only matters where you are going!" There is another saying that I think is equally profound, "There's no shame in being born with nothing, but it is a shame if you die with nothing or without having *done* anything!" Dr. Cindy Trimm is a woman who embodies both principles by continually reaching for greater heights of success and influence.

Dr. Trimm was born in Bermuda in a family of seven children. As a young child her father and mother split and her mother was left to support the family alone. The family struggled and ended up in abject poverty. Yet, even with few prospects for prosperity, Cindy knew that her destiny was bigger than her beginnings. She innately understood that it does not matter where you start, but where you finish.

Cindy made a commitment to be an excellent student and excelled in school to become a top student. She put herself through college and felt a call to help others. Thinking she could make a difference in politics, she ran for political office—and won! She went on to become one of the youngest senators in the Bermuda legislature. As she developed her political career, people started talking about her ascent as a potential high-level politician, but Cindy realized that there was a greater call on her life. She loved her job but realized that her most important call was not to be a potential prime minister, but to be an empowering minister of the gospel of Jesus Christ. Cindy left the prestige of national politics for the work of expanding God's Kingdom around the globe.

Dr. Cindy Trimm has gone on to become a world renowned speaker, empowerment specialist, and a prolific author. This is her latest book, which promises to be her biggest best seller yet!

This book teaches you how to prosper in a whole new way—a more holy and holistic way. Dr. Trimm explains the multiple facets of prosperity and how we can each achieve a life that maximizes every realm of prosperity available to us all. If you read this book, you will not be the same person when you finish as when you began. After reading this book, you will be inspired, encouraged, empowered, informed, and excited about your future.

Read this book with a pen in your hand, so you can capture the ideas that will be bursting into your consciousness. Share this book with your friends and your family members, so they too can prosper and be in good health—and so the water table of prosperous living will rise for all.

From this book you will understand as I do, that Dr. Cindy Trimm has made the commitment to help people globally realize that although they may not have started life with much, they can finish with much—and make a great difference by helping others prosper too.

May God bless you, and I pray that you live long and prosper!

Dr. Willie Jolley
Best-selling author, speaker

PREFACE

Dare to visualize a world in which your most treasured dreams have become true.
—Ralph Marston

Ancient wisdom from all parts of the world has long understood that you "become what you gaze upon." From prophets to philosophers, all agree that the power of vision, mindsets, beliefs, and perspectives are central to understanding the human experience—for each of us as individuals and for all of us collectively. This defines both our personal and societal way of being. How we see determines how we are as persons and as "a people." We are not as inclined to believe what we see as much as we are to see what we believe.

We ultimately become like that which we behold. What we focus on becomes our reality—our belief system about what is possible. We contract and expand according to the ebb and flow of expectations and our imagination. We may rise to the expectations of others, or fall based on the limited expectations we harbor within ourselves. Our mindsets govern our capacity to grow. Our sense of identity—or how we identify ourselves—is determined by the internal agreements we make about who we are, where we belong, and what we are capable of.

> *"What dominates our attention determines the direction of our life."*

We mirror what we identify with—we reflect what we see and focus upon. What dominates our attention determines the direction of our life.

It's true. The Bible tells us so. Jacob used this principle to breed the kind of sheep he wanted.[1] If it is true with animals that are not rational creative beings, can you imagine how true it is with humans? We are told in 1 John that we will become like Christ when we see Him.[2] The apostle Paul wrote that as we behold the glory of the Lord we are transformed into that same image.[3] What you behold you will become—and what you meditate upon you will give birth to. You could say that what grows in your mind will grow in your life.

This is why the life of the soul is so vitally important. It's why I wrote this series of soul books. It's why I wrote this book—so you could be transformed into "that same image"—that *"Christ in you, the hope of glory."*[4] We will be talking about how to create the necessary conditions for transformational growth—how to expand your capacity to be and do more—how to live a more prosperous life.

> *"You are always only one decision away from living the abundant life Christ promised."*

This is the third book in my soul series. The first book, *The 40 Day Soul Fast,* shows you how to detoxify and declutter your inner world. It takes you on a forty-day soul-cleansing journey to help you reboot from within. It introduces the forty characteristics of an authentic person that enable you to live with greater clarity, integrity, and freedom.

The second book, *Reclaim Your Soul,* focuses on how to take back your personal power in order to break free from self-sabotaging behaviors and toxic relationships. It discusses how to replace ineffective coping mechanisms with strategies that will protect you from common entanglements that ensnare your soul. Here we explore the emotional attachments and various types of soul ties that keep many bound, as well as the forty disciplines that will build the resiliency you need to get free and stay free.

Now, in this third book, we will talk less about what to move away from and more about what to move toward. Where before we learned about the impoverished soul, here we are focusing on the prosperous soul. We are doing less weeding and more planting. We are talking more about what *to* do rather than what *not* to do. The goal of our instruction is to help you live and love from a pure—and prosperous—heart.[5] What does "abundance" actually look like? What is true prosperity? What is real wealth? How do we forget the past and yet learn from it? How can we rewire our minds to create a more prosperous life?

It starts with making a choice—a single decision. You are always only one decision away from living the abundant life Christ promised you in John 10:10. You must decide to hope. You must decide to be joyful, to be grateful, to be expectant—to look for and see a more prosperous future. Can you envision it? Does it have the potential to hold your gaze? If not, what would? Dig deeper. Move past the "what" of desire to the more powerful "why" of drive. What drives you? Most people have no idea. They don't even know what it is they really want! I challenge you to search how many times in the New Testament Jesus asked those seeking His help, *"What do you want?"*

Today, as you read this, ponder what it is *you* really want. What's driving you? Ultimately, this is significantly more important than any consideration of what could be holding you back. As you will learn in the following pages, to prosper is to hope. The Lord told Jeremiah His plans were to prosper him—*to give him hope.*[6] It is the power of positive expectation—of a sense of possibility. The author of Hebrews wrote that hope is the anchor of our souls[7]—and it is what makes room for the joy that strengthens us.[8]

Create an image of what you want to see and then act "as if." What is that upward call *you* are pressing toward[9]—that's holding *your* gaze? How do you endeavor to *be*? Now, act as if it were so. As the ancient philosopher Socrates so famously said, "Endeavor to be what you desire to appear." And never lose hope—because you are always just one decision away from living the life of your dreams.

If you lose hope, somehow you lose the vitality that keeps life moving, you lose that courage to be, that quality that helps you go on in spite of it all. And so today I still have a dream.
—Dr. Martin Luther King Jr.

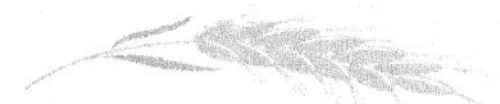

pros•per•ous \ˈpräs-p(ə-)rəs\ *adjective*

[Middle English, from Medieval Latin *prosperosus*, from Latin *prosperus*] 15th century

1: auspicious, favorable

2a: marked by success or economic well-being

b: enjoying vigorous and healthy growth: FLOURISHING[10]

pros•per \ˈpräs-pər\ *verb*

pros•pered; pros•per•ing \-p(ə-)riŋ\ [Middle English, from Anglo-French *prosperer*, from Latin *prosperare* to cause to succeed, from *prosperus* favorable] verb intransitive 14th century

1: to succeed in an enterprise or activity; *especially*: to achieve economic success

2: to become strong and flourishing; verb transitive: to cause to succeed or thrive[11]

INTRODUCTION

We must never stop dreaming. Dreams provide nourishment for the soul, just as a meal does for the body.
—Paulo Coelho,
The Pilgrimage

Joseph had a dream—and that's when the trouble started.

Or was it?

Have you ever considered what Joseph's life was really like before he began his epic journey toward greatness and world power? What did he struggle with before he left to find his brothers that fateful day, or even before his father gave him that famous coat?

Was there ever a time that he wasn't despised by everyone but his father? His mother died giving birth to his brother. His half-brothers had no use for him—in fact, they had come to hate him. Then he had a dream that he would be a great leader—so great, in fact, that even his father, mother, and brothers would bow down to him. What do you do with a dream like that when you're nearly the youngest and the most reviled among your siblings? Dreams like that—especially when they have a prophetic significance—can consume you, make you impatient to prove yourself to those who underestimate your potential.

Perhaps Joseph's problem was that he got too excited about the dream and not excited enough about the person he had to become to realize it. His immaturity in publicizing such a vision caused his brothers to think of him as delusional and arrogant. It drove them to despise and hate him all the more. And that seems to be when the *real* trouble started.

His brothers conspired against him and almost killed him. Can you imagine? At the last minute, one of them convinced the others to sell him as a slave to traveling nomads to avoid getting blood on their hands. He traveled in bonds to Egypt and was sold into an Egyptian household as a common laborer. If that wasn't bad enough, to add insult to injury, just as he was beginning to garner some respect, he was falsely accused of attempted rape and thrown into prison. For thirteen years of his life, Joseph lived as a slave and a convict—a dreamer and eventually an interpreter of dreams. Joseph had a greatness about him that invited "violent opposition" as described by Albert Einstein:

> Great spirits have always encountered violent opposition from mediocre minds. The mediocre mind is incapable of understanding the man who refuses to bow blindly to conventional prejudices and chooses instead to express his opinions courageously and honestly.

We all know the story of Joseph's overnight success when he went from prisoner to prime minister within a matter of hours. We love to talk about people who seem to succeed out of nowhere, but very seldom do we talk about the many nights they went to sleep with their dreams deferred, or the many years of character building that came before. We might think of these years as being his years of suffering. We might look on them as an unfortunate series of misunderstandings and injustices. We might think of them as lost years—years of adversity, hardship, oppression, and poverty. Wasted years. They may have been all of those things, but in looking at Joseph's life again recently, I came to a more powerful realization: *These were the years of Joseph's prosperity.*

Now you may say, "I beg to differ! Joseph didn't prosper until after those years! He didn't begin to prosper until he was put in charge of the nation. That was when he got the big house, lavish lifestyle, and fine family—large and in charge, living the life of his dreams! Those were Joseph's years of prosperity! Not when he was a slave and a convict!"

Yes, outwardly it may look like that—but we need to take a closer look at what prosperity really is. Prosperity has little to do with temporal success and more to do with spiritual resilience and the fortitude of the soul. Prosperity is the divine enablement that helps you overcome obstacles in order to fulfill a purpose—the capacity you need to maximize your potential to create change.

If you look at the definitions of *prosperous,* you will see the first word in its definition is *auspicious. Auspicious* has an interesting meaning. It is rooted in the word *auspice,* which indicates "a prophetic sign." Thus, to be *auspicious* means that things are going "according to favorable auspices," or prophetic signs or words. The Latin for "prosper"—*prospere*—is translated "according to expectation" or "according to hope"—and literally means "for hope." The word *prosperous* also means, "enjoying vigorous and healthy growth" or "flourishing." According to *Merriam-Webster, prosper* means "to become strong" as well as "to cause to succeed or thrive."

"Prosperity is the divine enablement that helps you overcome obstacles in order to fulfill a purpose—the capacity you need to maximize your potential to create change."

These are the roots or inner components of prosperity. Yes, to be *prosperous* also means "economic well-being," and to *prosper* also means "to achieve economic success," but I would submit to you that those are really outer manifestations of an inner condition—an internal state of wellness, growth, and expectancy—of what I believe is *true* prosperity. I have seen time and again that to be prosperous on the outside means nothing if you are not prosperous on the inside—and that being prosperous on the inside almost always leads to prosperity being evident from without. If you are prosperous on the outside only and lose your financial wealth, you are finished. If you are prosperous on the inside, however, and lose your financial wealth, you generally find a way to start over and rebuild it. Prosperity is a spiritual state that not only gives you psychological and emotional fortitude—even in the midst of the most adverse circumstances—but also the hope, faith, and love that never fails.[1]

For those who acknowledge prosperity merely by outward and financial measures, prosperity could be reduced to owning a big house, driving the latest new car, and living an opulent lifestyle. So many people enjoy that kind of life, but live with holes in their souls. If prosperity were simply a matter of "getting," anyone could borrow large sums of money or con their way into financial wealth through crooked "investment" schemes. Ambitious people could work long hours while ignoring their marriage and health, climb the corporate ladder by stepping on others, or any number of other ways people trade their souls to achieve "prosperity"—little by little, day by day doing whatever it takes to *look* prosperous. I call this the Ebenezer Scrooge Syndrome—living empty while facing death sitting on a pile of ever-diminishing wealth.

> *"True riches are not measured by what we own, but by what we give."*

Anyone who follows the news has seen where insider trading or ponzi schemes led to a quick fortune, even if it did eventually land the perpetrators in prison. But before they were caught, were they prospering? Consider the rich landowner who decided to build bigger barns in order to "eat, drink, and be merry"[2] without realizing he would die that very night. Such wealth creates a life that may feel good for a time but always ends the same—full of regret, broken relationships, or spending your hard-won accumulation of capital to regain the health you had taken for granted.

There is another kind of prosperity that, while it may require us to be more patient and intentional, is so much richer. It is a more pervasive prosperity—a prosperity rooted in wholeness. It recognizes that true prosperity is not about making a living but building a life. At the center is one's soul—one's core being—the source of vitality, potential, and contentment. It realizes that true riches are not measured by what we own, but by what we give—that the most rewarding balance sheet is not our net worth, but the extent to which we've positively affected the lives of others. It understands that true physical health comes out of spiritual strength and a thriving soul. It acknowledges that money is not an end unto itself, but a tool that can be used to extend God's love and His Kingdom. Prosperity is really summed up in the lives we touch, the influence we exert for the better, and the joy we experience as we learn, grow, create, and connect with others every day of our lives. It is about living in the fullness of Christ so we can do more toward making our communities safer, our governments more effective, our families healthier, and letting our "lights so shine" that through the provision of God, others might see our good works and glorify Him. It is about our *style* of living—versus a particular *lifestyle.* As Paul told Timothy, it is godliness that is *"profitable for all things."*[3]

This is why I believe that Joseph's thirteen-year experience as a slave and a prisoner were not lost years, but years of prosperity. They were years of transformational growth, capacity, and character building. They were years of honing his skills and refining his temperament. They were years of moral, ethical, and visionary leadership, as well as spiritual development. Had they not been, he never would have been ready when he was called before Pharaoh. He would not have had the insight to understand Pharaoh's dreams, or the wisdom to see what needed to be done to avert the disaster they foretold. Your current state of affairs has very little to do with where you currently are. Your challenges and crises have to do with where you are going—with your destiny. Like Joseph, you are

> *"God's favor prospers you with the provision to fulfill a purpose."*

a diamond in the rough, being refined by the heat and pressure of your circumstances.

The Bible tells us that God had favor on Joseph in the house of Potiphar and that everything he did there prospered.[4] As Pastor Steven Furtick of Elevations Church defines it, "The favor of God is the guarantee of His presence and the provision of His power to accomplish His special purpose in and through your life." Provision is provided to fulfill a purpose. Favor is needed when your future success is threatened by impending sabotage. It is in the midst of adversity that God provides what you need emotionally, psychologically, and spiritually in order to overcome the temptation to give up. Just because things may seem the opposite of what they should be if God were really causing your dreams, purpose, and assignments to come to pass, that doesn't mean all is not working for your good.[5] Whatever provision you've been given, in all its various forms, will enable you to fulfill a special purpose at this particular time—to *do good.*

Prosperity is about overcoming obstacles—political, cultural, economic, emotional, relational, etc.—so that when you arise out of hardship and setbacks, you come out better than you were before. That is what it means to prosper—to have the strength and resources *to do good* in spite of the bad that might be happening to you and around you. Prosperity allows you to say that no matter what, "I will bless the Lord at all times and His praise shall continuously be in my mouth, because I trust Him in the process."[6] Deuteronomy reminds us that it is God *"who gives you the strength to be prosperous."*[7] God's favor prospers us with the provision to fulfill a purpose—*"an abundance for every good work."*[8] It is not contingent upon our circumstances, experiences, opportunities, or background, it is *"but by the grace of God."*[9]

When Joseph was thrown into prison, he continued to grow, learn, and lead until he was running the place. God provided everything he needed. Every step along the way he prospered. If he had not, he would not have been the leader Egypt needed to save the Middle East—including Israel, Joseph's own family at the time—in its darkest hour. At that moment, Joseph's long season of "inward prospering" became seemingly sudden overnight "outward success." But it would not have been possible had he not come into deep agreement with who God said he was—aligning his entire sense of identity with who God had called him to be—regardless of his circumstances. Through it all, Joseph prospered knowing he was loved and accepted by God.

So, naturally, the question should arise within your heart, "When the apostle John writes in 3 John 2, *'Beloved, I pray that you may prosper in all things,'* does he mean in all material things, or in all circumstances?" I think of Romans 8:35 where Paul wrote that no thing—*"tribulation, or distress, or persecution, or famine, or nakedness, or peril, or sword"*—could separate us from the love of God. And in Philippians where he writes, *"Everywhere and in all things I have learned both to be full and to be hungry, both to abound and to suffer need."*[10]

> *An empowered life is a prosperous life.*

That said, 3 John 2 is more than a simple prayer, it is *the* key to true prosperity. *"May you prosper in all things and be in health, just as your soul prospers"* is at the center of the gospel message of empowerment. Jesus made that abundantly clear when He asked that quintessential question: *"For what will it profit a man if he gains the whole world, and loses his own soul?"*[11] What could be more disempowering than losing your soul?

An empowered life is a prosperous life, and a truly prosperous life only comes from a *prosperous*—"strong and flourishing"—soul that is, well, *prospering:* "enjoying vigorously healthy growth"—a *transformational* growth.

The prophetic "dream" God has given you may not be one that woke you in the middle of the night. It may not be a word that was given when someone called out your name from the pulpit to tell you God has a certain plan for your life. Those are wonderful things, but they should only confirm what is already in your heart. What God has planted in you is far more important than any external sign or signal. Your interests, your desires, and your skills and abilities—your inner drives and intrinsic motivators, all those things that get you enthusiastically out of bed in the morning—are clues to the dream God has for you. He has planted them deep within you, and if you seek Him, He will draw them out and turn them into the prosperity He so greatly wants for you.

What this means for most of us is that the joy and happiness we want out of life—the fulfillment that comes from discovering purpose and walking it out—is to be mined from the soul more than sought from the outside world. What starts within, leads to outside action; the prosperity of the soul emerges as an abundance others will see. While outside circumstances can sometimes pave the way to success, more often than not, it is the overcoming of them with integrity, inner strength, insight, and wisdom that leads to lasting blessings.

"Will you keep prospering on the inside until that steady preparation meets a "sudden" opportunity for you to change your world?"

Do you have a dream? Is there some burning desire you want to make a reality? Is there some issue in the world that tears at your heart every time you think about it? Those are clues to the dream and destiny God has planted inside of you. What will you do with them? Are you going to nurture them in the incubator of a prosperous soul, even when everything on the outside may be handing you hardship and setbacks just as it did Joseph? Will you keep prospering on the inside until that steady preparation meets a "sudden" opportunity for you to change your world?

By picking up this book and recognizing that God is calling you to do something great, you are drawing a line in the sand. There are going to be battles ahead. There are going to be stumbling blocks and difficulties. There are going to be times you get discouraged and wonder if your dream was more fantasy than prophecy. And although what God has put in your heart may seem difficult to accomplish, the pursuit of it is what makes life rich! There is no more meaningful adventure than the one He has called you to—no greater treasure than the one He has hidden within your soul.

Your all-access pass to the good life—the abundant life—is through the prosperity of your soul. It is what is inside of you—what you bring forth out of your heart—that *"determines the course of your life."*[12]

In the upcoming chapters we will look at the various aspects of the soul, how to make each of them grow and flourish, and then learn how to enjoy the fruit of what comes forth from your heart. We will investigate what true riches are and learn how to cultivate them. We will look at what it means to prosper in each of the key realms of life, and how to cultivate that abundance in your heart and nurture it out of your soul. We will learn about wholeness and reunifying the fragments of your life to live out what God has called you to do in every area.

This book has been designed—as are the other books in this series—to be used as an eight-week, forty-day study. Each week is divided into five days that explore the fundamental practices of prospering your soul. They are laid out so that you can read them on your own, do them as part of a weekly Bible study or Sunday School class—or just pick the book up, open it to a practice you need to undergird, and start prospering your soul.

Are you ready to begin digging for treasure?

A single day spent doing things which fail to nourish the soul, is a day stolen, mutilated, and discarded in the gutter of destiny.
—MICHEL FABER

Part One

A FUNDAMENTAL CHANGE OF HEART

For if anyone is a hearer of the word and not a doer,
he is like a man observing his natural face in a mirror;
for he observes himself, goes away, and immediately
forgets what kind of man he was
(James 1:23-24.)

Chapter One

THE HEART OF THE MATTER

If it is to be, it is up to me.
—William H. Johnson

A journey of a thousand miles begins with a single step. This is the day of your small beginning—one step toward a bold new way of life and living.

Now I realize that most of us don't want small change in our lives, especially if we have lived on this earth for a little while and aren't completely happy with where life has taken us—we want big change and we want it now. We want to quickly rise up the proverbial ladder of success, although even the ladder of success must be climbed one rung at a time! We want to impact lives on a national and international scale; we want to create innovations that will revolutionize industries; we want to leave a lasting impression on this world; we want our life—our only life on this earth—to matter! We want to leave a legacy that positively impacts future generations. We have big dreams—important dreams! We want to accomplish some great things—and all of that is very, very good. Yet any significant, world-changing endeavor begins with but the smallest seed of an idea...sown at the speed of thought, magnified by a single decision, set in motion by one single act.

If you look at history, you will see that big change rarely appears out of nowhere "overnight." Great innovations come as tiny seeds of insights that need to be cultivated, nurtured, and experimented with until they are brought from conception to manifestation—books that changed the literary world, technological advancements that altered the way we do life, medical breakthroughs that eradicated disease. Often these notions faced thousands of failures before "success" happened and was characterized as a *breakthrough.* Thomas Edison and the lightbulb provide a great example. He did thousands of trials before he found a filament that would last for more than a few seconds. When he finally did, the world was seen in a whole new light—literally.

Small companies take time to develop and grow into large, multinational corporations. They often require years of investment while only showing small incremental increases—or what may appear as devastating setbacks—before "suddenly" dominating the marketplace. As with all great ideas or products, so it is with our spiritual growth and development. One single activity alone is not a guarantee for success and prosperity. It is the accumulation of a series of right choices that turns the tides of failure into fortune, striving into thriving, and setbacks into success. We fail to maximize our potential because little things that can stabilize and prepare us for greater things are either overlooked, disregarded, despised, or viewed as unnecessary. In fact, I would go so far as to say that there is nothing more dangerous to a great idea than success that comes too quickly and easily.

"It is the accumulation of a series of right choices that turns the tides of failure into fortune, striving into thriving, and setbacks into success."

Think of it as building a beautifully lavish house on a weak foundation with inferior and insufficient plumbing. While needs are small and water flow is minimal, the people in the house can get along well enough fixing the occasional drip, putting out buckets to collect water, or tightening a leaky connection now and again. But what if the demands of the house suddenly require greater water pressure? Where there were drips before, there will now be jets of water shooting out in every direction!

Success brings its own demands and pressures. Spiritual, emotional, intellectual, professional, and financial growth requires that we exchange our childhood scripts for adult strategies. If not, we give away valuable personal power losing time, energy, money, and opportunities. Retrofitting a home is more expensive than building it right the first time. Likewise, many of us build our lives without much forethought of what it will take to grow into *"the measure of the stature which belongs to the fullness of Christ."*[1] We allow poor habits to undermine our foundations. We neglect to count the cost of completing the good work God has begun in our lives. We begin choosing the furniture before we have a blueprint! I pray this forty-day study will help you create a blueprint for the life of your dreams—and then lay a solid foundation to build it upon.

Pace for the Race

You have heard of young athletes who are awarded million-dollar signing bonuses when they go professional only to declare bankruptcy a few years later or lose their contracts because they can't control their mouths, fall into drug abuse, or wash out because they have no work ethic. You see it with movie stars who burn out too young, dying of drug overdoses because they didn't have the character to say "No"—or to live for something greater than their own pleasure. And you see it with businesses that have plodded along for years and suddenly have a big-selling product—they grow too fast, and when that product loses popularity just as suddenly, they find themselves in the red, laying off people, and often selling their business for the price of their debt. They end up with less than they had before their "success."

You may have thought in the past, "Why God—why don't You bless my finances? Why don't I ever get that promotion at work I am always praying for? Why isn't my ministry flourishing and influencing leaders like I dreamt it would? Why do I keep living hand to mouth when I see so many people succeeding who live only for themselves? Why do I have to go through what I'm going through? What am I doing wrong? I am sacrificing, paying my tithes, serving faithfully in church; why does life keep throwing me lemons? I'm tired of making lemonade!"

Time and again, when people make comments and ask me questions like these, I try to dig a little deeper. I ask them a few questions about their lifestyle and habits. When I do, I discover their plumbing—the infrastructure of their lives: their habits, their character, their organization, their people skills, and the like—is leaky and neglected. Their soul—the core of who they are—lies brimming with untapped potential, yet they remain blocked and unable to break through to all that God has for them. Why? Because if God suddenly released all He desired into their lives, it would not be a blessing; they don't have the spiritual foundation to bear the weight of the greatness, influence, and affluence God wants to pour out on them.

"Your success and prosperity are inextricably connected to the health of your soul."

When God blesses you by increasing your business, salary, or influence, it will create more pressure—just like creating greater water pressure for a home. If He blesses you, and your foundation and infrastructure are faulty, blessing you with increase won't feel like a blessing at all! God isn't in the business of "mixed" blessings. Believe it or not, God cares more about you as a person than He does about your calling. As counterintuitive as it may seem, your success and prosperity are inextricably connected to the health of your soul and entire being. It is His will that you prosper and be in health in as much as your soul prospers.[2] God is not going to bless you with more success than your personal infrastructure can handle—no matter how many lives it might help.

Your heavenly Father has no intention of burning you out, using you up, or wasting you—if any of those things are happening (mental anguish, broken relationships, isolation from family, stress-related illness, etc.), it is because you are out of alignment; you are not walking fully synchronized with God's will for your life—you are out of balance. With God-given success and prosperity comes *"righteousness and peace and joy in the Holy Spirit."*[3]

So, if you truly want to walk in the fullness of the abundant life God sent His Son to provide—if you want God to transform you into the world-changer you dream of being—then build your capacity by strengthening your spiritual support structures. Test the integrity of the inner foundation and the load-bearing beams of your soul. To go up, you must dig down; to go wide, you must go in. Check your plumbing. You'll need to shore up the infrastructure of your life in order to handle a much greater flow! You have to do what Joseph did while working in the dungeon—his own proverbial basement—you need to prosper your soul before God can prosper your life!

Think again of Joseph's dream. What do you think would have happened to Joseph if his dream of leadership and authority became a reality when he was seventeen? As it stood, he wasn't handling things too well with his brothers, and it appeared he was using his father's favor to avoid work more than do his part—otherwise why would he be delivering his father's instructions in his best outfit rather than his work clothes? The little we know about Joseph at that age seems to suggest he was a young man of leaky character and somewhat full of himself. He was not yet the man God could safely bless with the realization of his dreams.

So, Joseph gets sold into slavery. Suddenly he has no authority and all of his nice things are taken away—his designer garments, cushy job with all its perks, favor with his boss, and dinner with influential people, including his boss's family. He has a choice. He can grovel and complain that life is unfair and that he deserved better—that he is really a great man even though no one seems to recognize it—or, he could go to God and start changing in little, incremental ways. He could hone his skills and explore the last and greatest frontier, which is not outer space, but *inner* space. He could develop a better work ethic. He could become an industry-specific thought leader. He could express wisdom and become a difference maker as a problem solver. He could become a better team player. He could patch up his leaky character, mature spiritually, emotionally, intellectually, and socially so that he could handle hardships and challenges, thus becoming a man God could entrust with great responsibility and authority without it crushing him. In short, what he did was prosper his soul.

Prosperity Point

Do you want God to be able to trust you with more? What specific steps are you willing to take to see permanent change in your life? Do you want to be more prosperous socially, professionally, and financially? Do you want a healthier body, a healthier mind, and a healthier spirit? Success can certainly happen "overnight," but if it did, would it destroy you or propel you to the next level?

Oddly enough, the answer to all of these questions is rather simple, even though it can be far from easy. The answer is locked up in 3 John 2: *You will prosper and be in health in proportion to how you prosper your soul.*

Prosperity Thought

Each of us guards a gate of change that
can only be opened from the inside.
—Marilyn Ferguson

Chapter Two

A PROBLEM OF PARADIGMS

I do not understand what I do. For what I want to do I do not do, but what I hate I do (Romans 7:15 NIV).

Anyone who has ever sought to make serious change in his or her life has experienced the paradox that Paul describes in Romans 7:15. It starts with, "I know what is right, and it is not something that is currently a part or expression of my life. I *want* to change, but just can't seem to do so! I know *what* to do, but I don't do it!" There is a longing from deep within to be different, to be better. It may be a physical quality, such as losing weight, or it can be a character issue, such as being more generous, patient, or kind. It might be emotional, such as "I need to believe in myself and my abilities more," or it could be professional, whether being more focused, more productive, more punctual, or communicating more effectively. It might be social—a desire to reach out to friends more, connect more deeply within a community, or make more meaningful contributions. It could be that you want to create more emotional intimacy with your spouse or engage more deeply with your children as a parent. Or perhaps it is as basic as getting a better grip on your finances or managing your time better so you can exercise every day, or simply get the rest you need every night.

More.

Better.

But something keeps holding you back.

We address such issues in a number of ways—from merely thinking about them on occasion and saying, "I really need to get on that," to making to-do lists, or setting specific goals. Inevitably, something will come up; we'll get distracted by something more urgent, something easier to do, or that is simply more entertaining. Then, in a month or so, we think again about that change we desire and go through all of the same steps to nowhere. Time and again we find, *"what I want to do I do not do, but what I hate I do."*

Thus is the frustration of trying to change from the outside in.

As convicted as we may feel and as sincere as we try to be, prosperity rarely comes the way we want it; it takes discipline, persistence, and commitment. We might desire to be thinner, more respected, more loving and better loved by our families, more successful or financially stable—desires almost all of us have in one form or another—but such prosperity doesn't come by wishing for it. The person you are right now will always be the person you are right now—except, of course, a little older with more regrets—until you choose to embrace change at a fundamental level. Change doesn't start with forming new habits; it starts with asking the right questions, understanding what drives you, and clarifying for yourself the outcome you inherently desire. Like an Olympian training for the gold medal, you have to dig deep and discover what really moves you. What is your "why" behind the "what" you're hoping to achieve?

"Change doesn't start with forming new habits; it starts with asking the right questions."

It starts with changing the way you think about who you are, what you're capable of, and how you see your future self. Are you standing on a podium? Have you won the race? As Proverbs tells us, *"Carefully guard your thoughts because they are the source of true life"*.[1] Another translation states that how you think *"determines the course of your life"* (NLT)—whether you win or lose!

You, however, are your only competition when it comes to prospering as an individual. You can only become the best version of yourself—you will never be the best version of someone else. You can only win the race God has set before you by being the very best possible *you*. You might as well put your time in and get into God's life gym. Stretch those mental and spiritual muscles. Develop your prayer stamina. Learn how to compete with yourself and win! Never stop striving to beat your personal best! Go for the "gold" and see yourself proudly standing on your own podium of success!

"True prosperity is not so much about achieving traditional "benchmarks of success" as it is about being empowered."

But now I have to ask you: "How do you define success?" Arianna Huffington, author of *Thrive*, asserts that "the current model of success that equates success with burnout, sleep deprivation, and driving ourselves into the ground" is not working. She has created what she calls "The Third Metric of Success" that redefines success as "a focus on wellbeing, wisdom, wonder, compassion, and giving." As we will see in Chapter Four, these represent the overall hallmarks of empowerment. So I would assert that true prosperity is not so much about achieving traditional "benchmarks of success" as it is about being empowered—empowered to create, see things in a different light, think outside of the box, transform what is into what can be, consider every failure as an opportunity to learn, and every cost as an occasion to give selflessly. It's all about how you see.

One of Leonardo da Vinci's keys to creativity and innovation was what he called *saper vedere*, which simply means, "knowing how to see." To him, it meant he had to learn to recast the way he saw things if he was ever going to grasp whatever breakthrough he was chasing at the time. It spurred a systematic process he used to broaden his understanding of any topic that caught his fancy. In this way, he would virtually learn to "re-see" things, changing his perspective and learning to view them through a new, enlightening paradigm. He learned to look deeper and beyond what seemed immediately evident. He recognized that the problem—whether how to achieve a particular artistic expression or solve a physical challenge—was not really the problem. The problem was the paradigm through which he saw the issue. It would only be when he saw things differently—when he knew something he didn't before, when he was inspired in a way he had not yet been, or when he recognized some detail he had not yet noticed—that he could achieve the transformation he was pursuing.

This is exactly what Paul recognized and communicated in Romans chapters 7 and 8. Many quote Romans chapter 7 as a defeatist chapter and point to it saying even the great apostle Paul struggled with doing what he believed was right—but those who say that miss the paradigm shift in Romans chapter 8. Paul was not confessing his own struggles with living the type of life he wanted to live, he was expressing that when you want to change, you can't do it through outward rules and regulations—goals and resolutions. You can only do it with a fundamental change of perspective—a paradigm shift. You have to step out of the defeatism of Romans 7 into the possibilities of Romans 8:

> *There is therefore now no condemnation* [failure] *to those who are in Christ Jesus, who do not walk according to the flesh* [to outward "trying"], *but according to the Spirit* [the Source of inward change] (Romans 8:1).

In this statement, Paul is contrasting living according to the rules and regulations of the Law of the Old Testament—the long litany of mandates of which the Ten Commandments is only the beginning—with the new life that pours forth from the Spirit of God living within us. It is a contrast of trying to live by goals and resolutions versus embracing the life that comes from within when we feed, nurture, and discipline our souls. You don't need to discipline yourself to form new habits—what you need is to let new habits emerge as you prosper your soul.

Think of it this way: If you have a car that has a bad engine, giving it a new paint job, taking driving lessons, or simply changing the oil and filters isn't going to do you any good. Getting a new job, changing churches, or finding a new spouse isn't going to help get you where you want to go. What you need is a fundamental overhaul of the car's "soul," because your car is your means of transportation from where you are now to where you want to be. If you don't want to keep breaking down along the way, you have to get to the "heart" of the matter. Your vehicle needs to be overhauled from the inside out. Only when you pay the price to recalibrate the internal workings of your engine will you be able to get it into gear!

"*Your soul is the engine of your destiny.*"

Prosperity Point

Your soul is the engine of your destiny. It is what powers you toward the life you want to live. It is the "motor" that gives you the power to be the person you want to be every inch along your journey. Then, suddenly, with a new "heart," your outside changes will begin to make a difference. Grace will overhaul your engine. Your skill at praying will keep you safe; character will give your life new luster; favor will get you noticed; and the routine maintenance you allow the Holy Spirit to perform will bring the alignment needed to move you toward your dreams, bring you in view of your vision, and keep you on the road to maximizing your potential at optimal speed.

Are you ready to start your overhaul?

Prosperity Thought

I'm so grateful to Christ Jesus for making me adequate to do this work. Grace mixed with faith and love poured over me and into me. And all because of Jesus (1 Timothy 1:12,14 MSG).

Chapter Three

TRUE RICHES

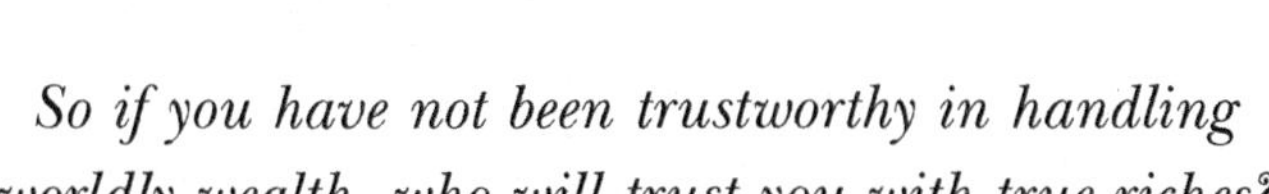

So if you have not been trustworthy in handling worldly wealth, who will trust you with true riches?
(Luke 16:11 NIV)

One of the strangest parables Jesus ever told is in Luke 16:1-8. The protagonist of the story, of all people, is an incompetent manager who through negligence and failure to discharge his duties misappropriated a good deal of his employer's wealth. During his annual performance review, the employer tells the manager he needs to come in with his records and account for any discrepancies. Knowing a "pink slip" was inevitable, the manager does an odd thing. After exploring his options and recognizing his propensity for laziness, being unwilling to do hard labor yet wanting to avoid welfare, he starts a collection agency and through solicitation, secures his boss's vendors as his first clients. He goes to his employer's creditors and begins working out deals with them to reduce their debts, thus ingratiating himself to them. Further squandering his employer's assets, he does whatever he can to *win friends and influence people,* so on the day he is fired, he can call in the favors he has done.

And so what happens? Does the employer get even angrier, reverse all of the decisions his manager has just made, and exile him to debtors' prison until he has repaid all he has squandered? Surprisingly no. Instead, Jesus tells us, *"The master commended the unjust steward because he had dealt shrewdly."*[1] Then Jesus added His own praise, *"For the sons of this world are more shrewd in their generation than the sons of light."*[2]

What? Is Jesus praising the man for being a crook? No. He is acknowledging his diligence in applying prosperity principles.

Perhaps some context will help. At the beginning of Luke 15, we are told that the religious community is accusing Jesus of hanging out with the wrong crowd: *"This Man receives sinners and eats with them."*[3] For the Pharisees and scribes, there was nothing worse than breaking bread with the wrong kinds of people. To them, to associate with someone was to be tainted by them.

To answer their accusation, Jesus tells four parables, ending with the Parable of the Corrupt Manager.

The first is the Parable of the Lost Sheep. To capture their attention, He tells them of the diligent shepherd who looks over the flock and realizes one of his one hundred sheep is missing. Being a good shepherd, he didn't say, "Oh, well. I still have ninety-nine left. I don't need to worry about that one." No, he left the ninety-nine to go find the one. Then he celebrated when he found the lost sheep. The religious listeners surely understood this story, for they were all well educated up-and-comers. They knew the value of a sheep and the importance of diligence.

Then Jesus tells the story of the Lost Coin. Here again, they must have empathized with the woman cleaning her home, knowing that every coin mattered to the welfare of her family. After all, what if it was lost? Would she then choose not to give money to the temple because God had taken her coin in another way? There were people depending on that money, after all (the priests in particular)! The religious leaders must have been able to identify with both of these people and felt they did the right thing in managing their affairs so conscientiously.

Then Jesus tells a story that is a little different. We know it as the Parable of the Prodigal Son, or you might call it the Parable of the Lost Son, to fit it in with the first two. The youngest son, hungry for the best of life, asks for his inheritance early so he can enjoy spending it while he is still in his prime. He, of course, foolishly squanders it on all the wrong things, ends up broke, and then has to find the worst type of job possible for a young Jewish boy—taking care of pigs. Finally coming to his senses, he realizes he would be better off working for his father than for the owners of these pigs who cheated their servants out of fair wages and decent living conditions. When he goes home, the father celebrates and receives him as his son rather than the fool who left him. The older brother objects when what will one day be part of his inheritance is wasted on his foolish brother. In response, the father chastises the older brother, pointing out that all that is on the farm will one day be his—and more as they continue to manage it and make it grow. What is one calf in comparison to the return of a lost brother?

If perhaps the religious leaders were made a little uncomfortable by this last parable—because they are obviously represented by the older brother—Jesus drives His point home with the Parable of the Corrupt Manager. Here is someone the religious leaders don't want to identify with at all—a dishonest and self-serving employee—and Jesus commends him for doing the most ridiculous of things! Accused of mismanagement, he mismanages even more to gain himself friends. Then, rather than being reprimanded, he is commended as wise!

Once again—*what?!*

Well, just in case they didn't get His point either, Jesus went on to explain:

> *I tell you, use worldly wealth to gain friends for yourselves, so that when it is gone, you will be welcomed into eternal dwellings. Whoever can be trusted with very little can also be trusted with much, and whoever is dishonest with very little will also be dishonest with much. So if you have not been trustworthy in handling worldly wealth, who will trust you with true riches? And if you have not been trustworthy*

> *with someone else's property, who will give you property of your own? No one can serve two masters. Either you will hate the one and love the other, or you will be devoted to the one and despise the other. You cannot serve both God and money* (Luke 16:9-13 NIV).

In God's eyes, what are true riches? From this passage, it is not hard to see: True riches are people, relationships, networks, and the friends we make. Real wealth is gained when we use our temporal means to restore lives to the Kingdom of God and glorify God in the process. When we meet Jesus at the gate of Heaven, the only worldly "wealth" that will come with us is the number of people we influenced toward Heaven and toward fulfilling their God-given purposes. Money, then, is not an end in itself, but merely a tool to be used toward garnering *true riches.*

"*Real wealth is gained when we use our temporal means to restore lives to the Kingdom of God and glorify God in the process.*"

And yet here we also find the paradox of wealth and prosperity. As an example, I heard about a group of college students who wanted to help solve world hunger. They sat in the cafeteria together with empty plates in front of them. They had a sign in the center of the table that said something to the effect of, "One out of every eight people in the world will go to bed hungry tonight." As they sat there and people walked by either ignoring them or giving them a look of approval, one of the students—now hungry himself—thought, "You know empty plates aren't going to feed anyone." From that simple revelation, he got the idea of hosting charity dinners for several hundred dollars a plate to help relieve poverty and hunger. By doing that, he helped far more people go to bed fed than he did by going hungry himself.

If we are going to help others, we need resources to do it—and money is one of the most transferable resources around. Poor people can empathize with one another, but only those with more than enough themselves can begin to come up with strategies to deliver others out of poverty. That is why I like to define prosperity as "the provision to overcome obstacles that prevent us from maximizing our potential and fulfilling purpose." It takes a crisis to expose our potential to solve the problems that will fulfill our purpose. Never allow the enemy to seduce you into playing the victim and *catastrophizing* your life.

What I think Jesus was saying in these four parables is that we can have only one of two relationships with money: Either we will serve it—we will spend all of our waking hours, our energy, our ingenuity, our resources, etc., to "get" it—or it will serve us; it will be a tool we can use to accomplish what God has put in our hearts to do on His behalf. The paradigm shift Jesus was communicating was that true wealth has more to do with touching people's lives and building relationships than it does with acquiring material possessions or improving our social status. Money is not for filling our lives with stuff, but for filling Heaven with people!

"True wealth has more to do with touching people's lives and building relationships than it does with acquiring material possessions."

Prosperity Point

The truly rich are those who have fully lived out their God-given purpose, changing the lives of the people around them for the better. True wealth is the relationships we make, the people we influence to become all God has called them to be, and knowing we have everything we need to become all He has called us to be. Worldly wealth is a tool to that end: "Provision to fulfill purpose." It means using the three things we have to invest—our time, our talents, and our treasure—to their fullest in the work of expanding the Kingdom of God.

Prosperity Thought

There needs not a great soul to make a hero;
there needs a God-created soul which will be
true to its origin; that will be a great soul!
—Thomas Carlyle

Chapter Four

THE EIGHT REALMS OF LIFE

What we set our goals on we give our attention to at the exclusion of other things. Setting goals can be dangerous because once you set a goal in one area, you've just excluded all others.
—Bob Harrison

It is interesting how often you hear the word "balance" as an important principle among success gurus, but how infrequently it is mentioned in the Bible. In fact, the only real references I have been able to find are in the book of Proverbs—the Bible's book of success wisdom. These references all seem to say something like this:

> *A just balance and scales belong to the Lord; all the weights of the bag are His concern* (Proverbs 16:11 NASB).

Now, I know I could finagle this verse into a life principle—and I have heard people do it—but to do so you really have to take it out of context. This verse isn't about balancing the different priorities in your life—like trying to find the right "balance" between home and work—but about being an honest merchant. If that is the case, is "life balance" a principle that the Bible overlooks? Or is it one that is inadvertently left out?

I think the answer to both these questions is "No." In the end, I don't think God is as concerned with "balance"—the idea of dividing your attentions evenly between the different realms of your life—as about *wholeness,* and more specifically, *wholeheartedness.*

As Robert Watson put it in his book, *Leadership Secrets of the Salvation Army:*

> Balance implies a static offsetting of forces. Children on a teeter-totter play at balance. They succeed when movement is arrested, when they are suspended, perfectly counterweighted. But that's not something we can hope for in real-life problem solving. We can't suspend things in space or time. We can't stop change. What we need is to connect with something that accommodates change, that, in fact, transcends it. We don't need to balance the fragments, to juggle all the separate people we imagine ourselves to be. We need to integrate them into a whole, moving in harmony with a transcendent, divinely connected purpose.[1]

I believe God is lovingly concerned about your priorities, but not in "balance" with one another. He wants to make them all an integrated whole by subjecting them to one overriding priority, namely, seeking first His Kingdom above all other things—in every area or realm of life—just as Jesus instructed in Matthew 6:33, *"Seek first the kingdom of God and His righteousness, and all these things shall be added to you."*

What does this mean on a practical level?

I'm glad you asked.

As human beings, we tend to fall into the ditches on one side of proper focus or the other; we become entirely consumed by our work or ministry to the exclusion of all else, or we get absorbed by whatever voice shouts the loudest in the present moment—what author Charles Hummel called the *Tyranny of the Urgent.* To put it more simply, we are either too myopic or too scatterbrained. When we make goals, they tend to be all in one or two areas—usually career and financial—or we set no goals at all, putting us at the mercy of whichever way the wind is blowing. When we do the first, we tend to succeed at work, but sacrifice our health or family to do it; when we do the latter, we tend to accomplish little or nothing that is important to us or connected with why God put us on the earth.

Thus, what I try to do is be aware of all of the major realms of life, and then seek to establish the Kingdom of God and put Jesus first *in each.* The realms of life are really tensions along four axis (and eight planes):

- Spiritual—Physical
- Emotional—Intellectual
- Vocational (or "Calling")—Financial
- Relational—Reputational

These represent four sets of near polar opposites (or opposite ends of a continuum), but we need each in our lives to have the full and abundant life God wants for us. The person who focuses on their physical world to the exclusion of the spiritual is missing the key element of the miraculous; the person who works for financial gain but in a field that does not speak to the desires of the person's heart will find only emptiness in his or her career. Of course, the person who follows the calling of his or her heart to the exclusion of having finances enough to provide for their family or live generously is going to fall short of being the caregiver and blessing the person should be. It is not a question of finding a balance between these pairings as we have already discussed, but of finding a place of wholeness where the needs of each realm are fulfilled. This may seem like a daunting task, but as we well know, nothing is impossible with God.

> *"True life-wholeness and abundance is achieved by seeking first His Kingdom and His righteousness in everything we do and pursue."*

What we want is the will of God in each area, *"on earth as it is in heaven."*[2] We must determine what God wants for us in each of these realms. Our objective should be to prosper in every area in accordance with the purposes of Heaven—how God wants us to fulfill His purpose for our life and the lives of those we love. True life-wholeness and abundance is achieved by seeking first His Kingdom and His righteousness in everything we do and pursue.

So, along with these eight primary realms that we will be discussing in the eight-week study ahead, there are also eight human drives that coincide with each realm: *the drive to be safe, to know, to be known, to bond, to grow, to be recognized, to achieve, and to acquire.* I find it interesting that according to psychologists, there are also eight hallmarks of an empowered person: *feeling loved, energized, supported, respected, and contributive: and having a sense of meaning, connectedness, and ownership.*

I've aligned the eight realms of life with the eight human drives and eight hallmarks of empowerment. Wholeness in the *spiritual* realm means we feel safe (or saved) by way of being loved by our Creator; the *intellectual* realm satisfies the drive to know and our longing for meaning; the emotional realm addresses our need to bond and feel connected; the *physical* realm is where our need to feel energized is satisfied by our drive to grow and improve; the *relational* realm is where our drive to be known satisfies our need to feel supported; the *social* realm addresses our need to feel respected and our drive to be recognized; the *vocational* realm satisfies our drive to achieve and to feel contributive; and the *financial* realm satisfies our drive to acquire and feel a sense of ownership.

> ***"God doesn't want us to live a life of balance between all the realms of life; He wants us to live fully in each and prosper."***

Thus, our forty-day study in Part Two is built around the eight realms of life, the eight human drives, and eight hallmarks of empowerment. In each of the eight weeks, we will look at one of these realms and the five practices crucial to prosper in each. By exercising these practices you will prosper your soul—thinking new thoughts, leveraging core drives, tapping into new motivations, and making better choices as a result. As the soul goes, so goes your life, and that is when we begin to *fully* realize God's will in every area.

Prosperity Point

God doesn't want us to live a life of balance between all the realms of life; He wants us to live fully in each and prosper. It's about *wholeness:* integrating the fragments of all the different people we imagine ourselves to be into one Kingdom-minded whole. The only way we can do that is to live by His strength, relying on His grace for every need. We do it by being fully present in each moment. We must look at each realm and make sure we have a picture of what God wants for us—what goals He wants to see achieved in each—and what it means to make each area prosperous.

Prosperity Thought

Your soul knows the geography of your destiny. Your soul alone has the map of your future, therefore you can trust this indirect, oblique side of yourself. If you do, it will take you where you need to go, but more important, it will teach you a kindness of rhythm in your journey.

—John O'Donohue,
Anam Cara: A Book of Celtic Wisdom

Chapter Five

THE CYCLE OF GRACE

Learn the unforced rhythms of grace
(Matthew 11:29 MSG).

We all make mistakes. We've all made bad decisions. We all, at some point, realize we are not where we want to be. We look back over the path we followed and recognize we took some wrong turns and made some selfish choices along the way. There comes a tinge of guilt, if not a feeling of condemnation that makes us question our worth. We wonder at how foolish we have been, and perhaps even think we have failed once and for all time. We feel trapped—like there is no way we will ever get ourselves out of the jam we have created. We feel defeated, we feel alone, we feel hopeless, and we might even feel like we can't do anything right. We may feel washed up and that there's nothing left in life to look forward to because we've lost our faith-grip on God.

> *"No matter what we have gotten ourselves into, God will give us what we need to get ourselves out."*

And that might be true, except for my two favorite words in the Bible: *"But God..."*

You see, when you think things are one way, and you're convinced you have come to the end of your rope, *"But God"* steps in, and suddenly things are really quite different. As Paul wrote to the Ephesians:

> ***But God,*** *who is rich in mercy, because of His great love with which He loved us,* ***even when we were dead in trespasses,***

> *made us alive together with Christ (by grace you have been saved), and raised us up together, and made us sit together in the heavenly places in Christ Jesus, that in the ages to come He might show the exceeding riches of His grace in His kindness toward us in Christ Jesus. For by grace you have been saved through faith, and that not of yourselves; it is the gift of God* (Ephesians 2:4-8).

This passage effectively says, "Even when we were dead in the water because of our mistakes and bad decisions, God made us alive again through what Jesus did by conquering the cross, raising us up with Him out of whatever mire or circumstances we might have gotten ourselves into, and setting us, in Christ, at His right hand in the throne room of Heaven." In other words, no matter what we have gotten ourselves into, God will give us what we need to get ourselves out. And what is it He gives us to accomplish that? There is only one word that really sums it up: *grace.* As Ephesians 2:8-9 just tells us:

> *For by* **grace** *you have been saved through faith, and that not of yourselves; it is the* ***gift of God****, not of works, lest anyone should boast.*

What is *grace?* It is a gift of God—not something we work to earn. Grace is different from faith. Faith is your grip on God. Grace is God's grip on you. When you lose your grip, He doesn't lose His.

In my mind, grace affects us in three different ways:

1. Grace restores us into an authentic relationship with Christ our Savior and a place of right-standing before God through the enabling power of the Holy Spirit,

2. Grace enables us to maximize our potential, equipping us to fulfill our daily assignments and walk out

the plan of God for our lives according to His divine timetable, and

3. Grace helps us to discharge our moral and ethical responsibilities as citizens of this world as it overflows from our life to touch the lives of others.

Understanding these three distinct aspects of grace is fundamentally important for connecting with God not only for salvation but also for living the kind of abundant life all desire to live this side of Heaven.

While the grace of God is freely offered, you have to step in and accept it in order for it to do you any good. You have to actively receive it. When you accept Jesus as your Lord and Savior and believe that God raised Him from the dead, you step into the first work of grace that opens the doors for you to be readmitted into God's presence, into His throne room, and with His ear turned to hear your petitions. This is granted when you are "saved"[1] or "born again"—where you were once spiritually separated from God, but now have open access and right standing, so you can come before Him for any reason at any time.[2]

That is something you have to accept by faith and not by feeling. The enemy's most successful ploy to keep you from touching the world with God's love and goodness is to make you *feel* like you are not worthy—that you don't actually have access to God, and even if you did, you have a lot of cleaning up to do before you can approach Him. But that is not the truth. While you may certainly need to confess some mistakes and indiscretions, if you have given your life to Him, sin cannot keep you from God's presence. Thus, when you feel you need to make a course correction in your life because you have wandered off the path He laid out for you, you don't have to grovel and do penance before you can have His attention again—you just have to repent—turn your heart back to Him, confess, and pray. As the Scriptures tell us:

> *Let us therefore come boldly to the throne of grace, that we may obtain mercy and find grace to help in time of need* (Hebrews 4:16).

This first work of grace—that gives you access to God the Father whenever you want or need it—leads to the second type of grace, which is tailored to whatever your need is at the moment. It is the grace that equips, the grace that enables, the grace that gives insight, or the grace that creates breakthrough. It is the grace that comes just as you need it for the situations you face in life. While this kind of grace is also freely given, it doesn't do you much good if you are not walking in step with the Spirit of God. It comes with learning the rhythms of grace, which override the limits of your flesh. As Paul told the Corinthians:

> *"God's rhythms of grace override the limits of your flesh."*

> *God is able to make all grace abound toward you, that you, always having all sufficiency in all things, may have an abundance for every good work* (2 Corinthians 9:8).

In many ways, grace is what this book is all about. You must learn to walk in constant grace so that you not only have what you need from God to succeed and prosper in any given moment, but so that His grace would overflow from you to every life you touch. The readings for the next eight weeks will give you the practices that enable you to stay in touch with the grace you need every minute of every day; and as you do this in each of the different realms of life, you will experience God prospering your soul.

Prosperity Point

God's grace provides you with access to Him—and right standing before Him—as His representative to make requests on behalf of yourself and others. Grace also becomes whatever it is you need—strength, character, insight, inspiration, equipping, wisdom, etc.—to accomplish the purpose for which He put you on the earth. This empowering aspect of grace isn't a one-time endowment, but something you receive little by little, day by day, and moment by moment as you walk in step with His Spirit. It comes out of a life of communing with God in everything you do—living in a continuous rhythm of pursing His presence by asking Him how best to fulfill His purpose in every area of your life; seeking Him for His empowerment to truly prosper and for *all* you need to succeed in touching others with His love and truth.

Prosperity Thought

Excellence is an art won by training and habituation.
We do not act rightly because we have virtue or
excellence, but we rather have those because we
have acted rightly. We are what we repeatedly do.
Excellence, then, is not an act but a habit.
—Aristotle

Part Two

40 PRINCIPLES AND PRACTICES FOR A MORE PROSPEROUS LIFE

For we are God's masterpiece. He has created us anew in Christ Jesus, so we can do the good things he planned for us long ago (Ephesians 2:10 NLT).

Week One

SPIRITUAL PROSPERITY

No pessimist ever discovered the secret of the stars, or sailed to an uncharted land, or opened a new doorway for the human spirit.
—Helen Keller

Day One

GOD'S WORD

Every part of Scripture is God-breathed and useful one way or another—showing us truth, exposing our rebellion, correcting our mistakes, training us to live God's way. Through the Word we are put together and shaped up for the tasks God has for us
(2 Timothy 3:16-17 MSG).

In Mark 4, Jesus tells the story of what you might think is a rather foolish farmer.

It seems that this man took his seed and flung it all over the place. As he was tossing it every which way, some landed in the street, some on stony ground, some in places full of weeds, and some, quite accidentally it seems, landed on fertile soil. A smarter farmer, you would think, would sow all of his seed in the last type of soil where the roots could grow deep, find nutrients, and the resulting plants would thrive. Good farmers know good soil, after all. But then again, I don't think this story is about the farmer, or the seed. I think this story is about the soil. Jesus seems to be asking His listeners, "What kind of soil are you?"

The first type of soil Jesus spoke of was much like concrete. The seed—or the Word of God in this case—sits on the hard surface, baking in the sun, with no chance of putting down roots. When a gust of wind comes along, or a pesky bird arrives to pick at it, the seed is snatched away. There is no possibility of the seed penetrating the soil's hard outer crust. "The Bible's an old book, full of old myths," this person might think. "What does it have to do with the world today? Why should I waste my time?" So the Word sown in such soil cannot take root, and the potent seed sown there does no good at all.

The second type of "soil" is shallow and rocky. The Word is received and begins to sprout roots—but then hits something hard and can go no farther. There's a rock under the surface that the roots can't penetrate. If you looked at these people on the surface, you would think they are good soil, but inside there are things blocking their growth. They may have self-esteem issues. They may have hurts or abuses in their past that they have buried. They may have soul ties that act like anchors, holding them in place and keeping them from moving on.[1] There may be bitterness or envy in their souls that dry up the roots before they are able to take hold. These inner issues keep the Word from blossoming and profiting them. They will not be good soil until they dig those rocks out of their lives.

Others are good soil, but they refuse to give the Word the place of preeminence that will allow it to multiply. You see, along with the Word, they have planted sundry interests, goals, and hobbies that distract their attention and displace their interactions with God. Their priorities are misaligned. They don't *"seek first the kingdom of God and His righteousness"*[2] in every realm of their lives, but rather allow *"the cares of this world, the deceitfulness of riches, and the desires for other things"* to enter in and choke *"the word, and it becomes unfruitful."*[3] They pile their plates with activities for their kids, the demands of their jobs, entertainment, following their favorite sports teams, socializing with friends, even church activities, all of which take their focus off of seeking intimacy with God and prospering their souls. These distractions might be perfectly acceptable things, but they are not what is best—they are not what God is calling individuals to grow in.

The last type of soil is fertile soil where the roots of the Word sink deeply and *"bear fruit: some thirtyfold, some sixty, and some a hundred."*[4] This type of soil rarely just happens. As with the most fertile soils—or even souls—they must be cultivated. Good soil has to be worked. You have to clear the brambles and dig out the rocks. You have to break up the fallow ground. You have to till the soil and fertilize it so that it will be rich and productive. You have to *prosper* the soil so that the Word can bear abundant fruit.

Our souls are the soil in which God plants the seed of His Word—not only the words we find written in Scripture, but also the individual words of prophecy or admonition we hear through His ministers. The fertility of the soil of our soul is in direct proportion to how much we have worked to prosper our spirits. Not only that, but Jesus tells us that this parable is the key to understanding everything else that He wants to teach us! Jesus said:

> *"Our souls are the soil in which God plants the seed of His Word."*

> *Do you not understand this parable? How then will you understand all the parables?* (Mark 4:13)

Thus this parable is a key to the prosperity of your soul. How do you regard the Word of God? Is reading and studying the Bible an integral part of your daily routine? What place do Scripture and the instructions of God hold in your mind and heart? Do you believe them and live by them, or are they more like guidelines you can bend when you want to do something else? Are you a little unsure if the Bible truly is the Word of God? Or are you the type of person who declares, "The Bible says it, I believe it, and that settles it!"

The Bible is not just another book. It is alive[5] and multifaceted. It is not only *"profitable for doctrine, for reproof, for correction, for instruction in righteousness, that the man of God may be complete, thoroughly equipped for every good work,"*[6] but it is inspiration, understanding, and insight. When you study the Bible in light of your cares and issues, it opens your heart for the Holy Spirit to speak to you. You may be reading about forgiveness, and the Holy

Spirit will use that to give you the conviction and words you need to speak to an offended friend, colleague, or relative. You may be reading the Psalms, praising God's majesty, and He will give you insight into solving a problem with something you are designing at work.

I recently read a story that enforces the importance of daily Bible reading:

> A circuit-riding preacher entered a church building with his young son, and dropped a coin into the offering box in the back. Not many came that Sunday, and those who did didn't seem too excited about what was said. After the service, the preacher and son walked to the back, and he emptied the box. Out fell one coin. The young boy said, "Dad, if you'd have put more in, you'd have gotten more out!"[7]

So I ask you, what is the place of the Word of God in your life? Do you give it the respect that you should? How much time have you put into studying the Bible? Do you read and study it regularly looking for insight into who God is and what He has planned for you? Do you focus on it attentively when you read it—or when it is read to you in a Bible study or as part of a sermon—so that God can speak to you through it? If you put more time and attention into pursuing God's Word, you will get more out!

> *"What is the place of the Word of God in your life?"*

Prosperity Point

Prosper and cultivate your soul so it is fertile soil for what God wants to sow there. He gives you the seeds of His Word not only so you may bear fruit, but also so that you can discern how He is speaking to you. God's Word is a legal document that He stands behind. In fact, the Bible states, *"You have magnified Your word above all Your name."*[8] Do you magnify the veracity of His Word in the same way?

Prosperity Thought

The Word we study has to be the Word we pray. My personal experience of the relentless tenderness of God came not from exegetes, theologians, and spiritual writers, but from sitting still in the presence of the living Word and beseeching Him to help me understand with my head and heart His written Word. Sheer scholarship alone cannot reveal to us the gospel of grace.

—Brennan Manning,
The Ragamuffin Gospel

Day Two

PRAYER

Spirituality without a prayer life is no spirituality at all, and it will not last beyond the first defeats. Prayer is an opening of the self so that the Word of God can break in and make us new. Prayer unmasks. Prayer converts. Prayer impels. Prayer sustains us on the way. Pray for the grace it will take to continue what you would like to quit.

—JOAN CHITTISTER,
In a High Spiritual Season[1]

In many ways, prayer is to the spirit what breathing is to the body—and according to the apostle Paul, it should happen just as often.

Certainly we should set aside specific times to pray. Whether you keep a prayer journal, pray over a set of Scriptures, or read from a series of proclamations, taking just fifteen minutes every morning to acknowledge *Who* is first in your life versus *what* is first will transform your day. We all need to take time every day to lay our requests before the throne of Heaven and listen to what God has to say to us. Prayer, after all, is a dialogue, so we should take as much time to listen as we do to speak, even if God seems quiet. I find He answers much more with His presence than He does with words—and in that presence over the years, I have found more answers than I ever imagined possible.

Paul told us that we should *"pray without ceasing"*[2] and that we should be *"continuing steadfastly in prayer."*[3] If you are like me, you look at a world that has so many concerns and issues, and you meet so many people who need a touch from God, that you might feel you should do nothing but stay in your prayer closet 24/7. It can be so overwhelming, in fact, that you may be reluctant to pull aside to pray *at all* because you're not sure where to start—let alone end!

However, God never intended prayer to be a burden. Instead, it is a way to grow closer to Him and understand His heart. He meant it as a way for you to cast *"all your care upon Him, for He cares for you."*[4] He meant it as a way for you to invite Him to invade your space as well as come before Him with the issues that trouble you, invading His. Prayer is not a soliloquy. Prayer is communicating with God in a dialogue—meaning it goes two ways. It is being in His presence and inviting Him into yours. Your place of prayer is your place of power. There is no situation, no family member, no government, no disease, no thing or person who is off-limits or out of the reach of prayer.

How can you neglect such an incredible opportunity—or confine it to just a few minutes of your day?

Do you know what Google Hangout is? It is an online video chatting system where you can communicate on the Internet; however, it is intended to be a place where friends log on and just "hang out" as they do whatever they are doing in front of their computers. In a lot of ways, God's invitation to us is to pray like that—it is God inviting us to hang out with Him. That's the place where real prayer begins.

> *"Your place of prayer is your place of power."*

In other words, prayer is as simple as practicing the presence of God—you get to hang out with Him in the throne room and not earth's chat room. In prayer, you have the ear of the Creator of Heaven and earth, who said that all things are possible if you believe. Prayer gives you the confidence of knowing that you have His ear no matter what is concerning you—while He has your ear whenever He has something to tell you. It is as much about the short breath prayers we lift up throughout our day—"Lord, help me through this," "Father, touch that angry man with Your love and peace," "Oh God, be with my child today as she takes her test," "Please help my boss come to know You"—as it is attending prayer meetings or interceding for hours about particular issues.

In addition to hanging out with Him, we can also "instant message" Him with whatever tweaks our heart at any moment of the day or night. Prayer takes place at the speed of thought! As you breathe out your requests before God in prayer, take time to breathe back in from the Spirit of God. Listen. Focus on the truth that God is right there with you in the moment. Inhale His goodness and the grace you need. Release your concerns into His hands and breathe back in His peace and faith for what you face. Out goes the anxiety, and in comes His joy, confidence, and hope. Prayer is saying, "God, You are here in this moment. You are here with me and promised to never leave me or forsake me. I trust You, Lord."

> *"Prayer is the doorway between God's home and yours. His door is always open—is yours?"*

I think prayer pleases God more than any other discipline of our faith. Why? Because God likes hanging out with us more than we could ever imagine.

Prayer is not a chore, although for many Christians, that is all it may ever be—but it doesn't have to be that for you! And that is certainly not how it is intended to be. You can transform prayer from a perceived duty or chore into an exciting way of life.

Prayer fitness is much like physical fitness. Everyone knows if you're out of shape physically, you will go through a phase of real and painful struggle to get back into shape before enjoying the benefits of a healthier lifestyle. If you're overweight, you will struggle through a difficult time of changing how you eat, disciplining your appetites, and making time to exercise every day before you will enjoy a stronger, fitter body. So it is with prayer.

To build a stronger prayer life, you must discipline yourself to pray.

If your prayer life is out of shape, weak, and flabby, you will tire easily—you will get bored, discouraged, and perhaps a little sore. Every time you do pray, however, you build stronger spiritual muscles. It's a matter of consistency. Just like you wouldn't expect to run ten miles if you've never run one—so it is with prayer. Doing a little every day—rather than nothing at all—will cause you to do a little more and then a little more, every time you put on your tennis shoes or enter your prayer closet.

Here's a simple prayer you can pray right now to jump-start what I hope will become a life-transforming routine:

> *Lord, help me to exercise my prayer muscles. I trust that You will bring me to a place of greater spiritual strength and power as I make time to pursue Your presence each and every day. Thank You for being my personal trainer as I endeavor to make this a priority and way of life. Amen.*

Praying is the only way to pray. When you begin to experience how prayer really works and what prayer actually does, you will want to make it a lifestyle.

Prosperity Point

If you were going to learn about a famous person, which would you choose to do: A) listen to someone else talk about them, B) read a book about them, or C) meet them? We learn about God in the same way: By listening to sermons, reading books about Him (including the Bible), and spending time with Him. All are important. All add perspectives to our knowledge of a person, but nothing beats talking with them face to face—or visiting them in their home. Prayer is the doorway between God's home and yours. His door is always open—is yours?

Never forget the unique privilege that prayer is, nor the privilege of practicing it in every moment by communing with God with you throughout your day. The great preacher Charles Spurgeon once said, "Prayer...is an art which only the Holy Spirit can teach us. Pray for prayer. Pray until you can really pray." If you pray regularly and practice the presence of God wherever you go or whatever you do, it will make the spiritual world just as alive to you as the physical world—and when that is true for you, life becomes a more exciting adventure!

Prosperity Thought

Don't fret or worry. Instead of worrying, pray. Let petitions and praises shape your worries into prayers, letting God know your concerns. Before you know it, a sense of God's wholeness, everything coming together for good, will come and settle you down. It's wonderful what happens when Christ displaces worry at the center of your life (Philippians 4:6-7 MSG).

Day Three

MEDITATION

Summing it all up, friends, I'd say you'll do best by filling your minds and meditating on things true, noble, reputable, authentic, compelling, gracious—the best, not the worst; the beautiful, not the ugly; things to praise, not things to curse. Put into practice what you learned from me, what you heard and saw and realized. Do that, and God, who makes everything work together, will work you into his most excellent harmonies (Philippians 4:8-9 MSG).

When I talk about meditation, I am not talking about putting on some comfortable clothes and sitting on a mat in the lotus position. What I am talking about are the thoughts you think throughout the day. In 1 Timothy 4:15, the apostle Paul advised his protégé Timothy to *meditate* on the gifts he had received from God; on his calling; on his preaching, reading, and doctrine; as well as his being *"an example to the believers in word, in conduct, in love, in spirit, in faith, in purity."*[1] *Vine's Complete Expository Dictionary* tells us that *meditate,* in this sense, means, "to attend to, practice...be diligent in...to ponder, imagine." It is the activity of a dreamer or anyone hoping to accomplish great things. We not only have to plan, but we have to spend time pondering who God has called us to be, how He has equipped us, what He has ahead of us, and how others will be affected by everything we do. We need to fill our mind with the possibilities of God and not the limitations of this world; *"For as* [a person] *thinks in his heart, so is he."*[2]

Through meditation we are able to honor the capacity of the human spirit and the potential buried within our souls. The soul—one's mind, will, and emotions—is a wondrous place and the seat of all human creativity, innovation, and insight. According to Dr. Vilayanur S. Ramachandran, Director of the Center for the Brain and Cognition at the University of California, San Diego, our minds are much more than most of us realize. Your mind impacts the impulses of your brain.

> [Your brain] is this three pound mass of jelly you can hold in the palm of your hand. It can contemplate the vastness of interstellar space. It can contemplate the meaning of infinity, ask questions about the meaning of its own existence, and about the nature of God. This is truly the most amazing thing in the world—it is the greatest mystery confronting human beings. How does this all come about?
>
> The brain, as you know, is made up of neurons. There are 100 billion neurons in the adult human brain and each neuron makes something like 1,000 to 10,000 contacts with other neurons in the brain. Based on this people have calculated that the number of permutations and combinations of brain activity exceeds the number of elementary particles in the universe.[3]

Quite often as human beings, we think we are limited. We look at the stumbling blocks before us, the disadvantages life has handed us, or the deficiencies in our abilities or education. Yet, by making the proper connections in our minds and brains, there are more possibilities of who we can become than there are

> *"Through meditation we are able to honor the capacity of the human spirit and the potential buried within our souls."*

"elementary particles in the universe"—that isn't speaking of the number of molecules, but the number of things that make up all of the molecules *in the universe.*

Who you are and who you will become throughout your life is about the connections that are made in your brain as you think and learn—as your mind prospers. There are connections that you can make that no one else in the history of the world has ever made before. There are insights to be realized that will yet revolutionize the earth. The printing press—the invention many recognized as the greatest invention of the second millennium—was not made of anything new. It was the combination of several components that already existed, but no one had thought to combine them into one machine before. The screw press had been invented to crush grapes in order to make wine or squeeze olives to make oil. The Chinese had known about moveable type for years, even though it was cumbersome and less efficient than copying text by hand. Paper, of course, had been around for centuries, but all books up to that point were "printed" by scribes, brushstroke by brushstroke, as they painstakingly and meticulously copied older editions. Separately, none of these technologies were really very efficient, but when they were combined, they were able to mass-produce books as never before. Suddenly knowledge could travel and be preserved. Literacy and libraries meant that each generation no longer had to "reinvent the wheel" for themselves, but could stand on the shoulders of previous generations continuing from where they left off rather than starting from scratch.

We also see the phenomenal power of thought in the lives of men such as George Washington Carver, who, though born a slave in the midst of the Civil War, transformed the South with a simple prayer, "Great Creator, why did You make the peanut?" Then he turned his mind to discovering everything that could be made from this trash crop. (At the time, peanuts were planted to replenish the nitrates in the soil where cotton was being grown.

After a number of years, cotton so depleted the soil of nitrates that the farmers would plant peanuts to revitalize it. Then having little or no use for the peanuts, they were discarded. Farmers had to go without a cash crop in those fields for each season they planted peanuts, so Dr. Carver determined that if he could find a use for the peanut, it would provide those farmers with a source of income.)

Through his work, Dr. Carver found over 300 uses for the peanut by breaking it down into its parts, and then recombining them one by one, in groups, and under different conditions of heat, pressure, etc. He patented two of them giving him all the finances he needed for the remainder of his life, while the rest he left free to anyone who wanted to profit from them. It created extra income for tens of thousands.

> *"Your mind will only prosper if you meditate on the "dos," the "cans," and the "possibilities.""*

We have but to look at any invention or innovation. They were all born from the prosperous mind of human beings as God helped them connect the dots for the good of all. Some of the greatest thinkers, from Isaac Newton to R.G. Letourneau, were men of both faith and science who constantly asked God to increase their understanding and improve their world. By mixing their thoughts about God with the questions that puzzled them, their meditations transformed lives. It's an issue of mind over matter.

Prosperity Point

What thoughts do you allow to linger in your mind as you go about the business of living each day? Are you pressing God for greater insight and understanding? Are you asking big questions and meditating on His promises? On the possibilities of His universe? Are you hungry for new connections and innovations in whatever field you work: Arts and entertainment, business, education, family, government, media, or religion? Or are you poisoning your soul, sucking on bitterness and nursing hurts? What touches your heart? What would you do if money were not an issue? What is happening around you that is *"true, noble, reputable, authentic, compelling, gracious"*? Your mind will only prosper if you meditate on the "dos," the "cans," and the "possibilities."

Prosperity Thought

Such as are your habitual thoughts, such also will be the character of your mind; for the soul becomes dyed with the color of its thoughts.

—Marcus Aurelius,
Meditations

Day Four

FASTING

This is the kind of fast day I'm after: to break the chains of injustice, get rid of exploitation in the workplace, free the oppressed, cancel debts. What I'm interested in seeing you do is: sharing your food with the hungry, inviting the homeless poor into your homes, putting clothes on the shivering ill-clad, being available to your own families. Do this and the lights will turn on, and your lives will turn around at once (Isaiah 58:6-8 MSG).

To fast is to consecrate yourself, often by denying yourself something, in order to more fully focus on Heaven. People usually think of going without food or water when they think of fasting, but it can actually take many different forms. Fasting is about cutting away and suspending a particular activity so that it is replaced with some other activity. You don't have to simply eliminate the consumption of food—you can also fast habits, other daily activities, such as watching TV or surfing the Internet, or anything you do regularly that you feel has become a distraction, or even an addiction, keeping you from "seeking first the Kingdom." For the length of the fast, this gives you a laser-like focus on the things of Heaven. Such times pull you closer to God, help you better discern His voice, and prosper you spiritually as you remind your brain and body to be submissive to spiritual things. Fasting strengthens your self-control in doing what God has called you to do and can bring clarity in following Him. It can also bring breakthrough in any area where you may feel trapped or stagnant. If practiced properly, fasting can bring times of rapid growth and spiritual insight.

There are various types of fasts. You can do an absolute fast—no food, no liquids—but you should only do such extreme fasts if you feel called by God to do so, for a short period of time, no longer than three days. These are hard on your body and can have unhealthy physical ramifications. Absolute fasts don't necessarily have more beneficial effects than any other type of fast, either. The point, after all, is to seek God, not inflict suffering or injury on yourself.

> *When we fast, we put ourselves into the hands of the Father so He might prune away the things that are hindering our success.*

There are also water-only and liquid-only fasts (where you might drink broths or juices to keep up your strength). Then there is the "Daniel Fast," which is traditionally a fast where you avoid eating anything but fruits and vegetables and drink only water (though you will find various interpretations of the Daniel Fast in different publications and on the Internet). You can also go on a cleansing fast where you eliminate toxic foods such as sugar, inorganic (most factory-raised) meats, and anything artificially flavored, pre-packaged, or processed; or you could simply give up one meal—skipping lunch, for example, to go somewhere and pray instead of eating—or you can fast one day each week for a season. You can go on three-day, seven-day, twenty-one-day, or forty-day fasts, or any of the numbers in between (the lengths mentioned, however, are found in various places of the Bible).

You can also fast something during the forty-days leading up to Lent, such as sweets or coffee, or things you feel distract you, such as television, social media, video gaming, etc. The thought, again, is that you replace the habit or activity with focus on God, so that whenever your thoughts naturally turn to that activity or habit, you are reminded to pray, meditate on Scripture, worship, or work from a Bible study.[1] People often go on fasts in order to break the power of certain habits over their lives. Fasting can be used to overcome addictions, such as smoking, drinking, gambling, or any other thing that has a hold on you and threatens your life, your relationships, or your livelihood.

In many ways, fasting is practicing a certain thrift-of-the-spirit. It is looking at your time, energy, and attention and determining what is the best way to "invest" them. It is a way of getting together with God and letting Him prune away the things you don't need in your life as the Master Gardner Jesus describes in John 15:1-4:

> *I am the true vine, and My Father is the vinedresser. Every branch in Me that does not bear fruit He takes away; and every branch that bears fruit He prunes, that it may bear more fruit. You are already clean because of the word which I have spoken to you. Abide in Me, and I in you. As the branch cannot bear fruit of itself, unless it abides in the vine, neither can you, unless you abide in Me.*

When we fast, we put ourselves into the hands of the Father so He might prune away the things that are hindering our success—all so we can be more fruitful and prosper.

But it is not just about our relationship to Heaven. Proper fasting should result in action, not only in the spiritual realm, but also in the natural world. After all, every battle is won first in the spirit before that victory manifests in the natural. Isaiah 58, among other passages of Scripture, tells us that what is gained in fasting should spill over into our day-to-day lives in the form of justice—how we love others as God has loved us; mercy—how we proactively forgive just as God has forgiven us; and faithfulness—how we respond to God despite circumstances, just as He responded favorably to us while we were yet sinners. If we do not manifest these virtues in our lives, then our fasting is motivated by something other than seeking His will and expanding His Kingdom.

Before you begin a dietary fast, do some research on how to maintain your health and the integrity of your time with God. If you have health concerns, consult your doctor before you begin. All of these will help you keep "the main thing the main thing" as you fast.

PROSPERITY POINT

True fasting cannot take place if it doesn't change our hearts as well as our bodies. It needs to affect how we treat others as well as what we do about the issues of injustice, oppression, and prejudice that affect so many in the world today. It should facilitate our intimacy with God so we can become "vessels of honor,"[2] *vesseling* His will in the earth through our lifestyles and prayers. Fasting reminds us to be hungrier for God than we are for the things of this world, even the food we need to live. It reminds us to put spiritual things first and to seek God in every concern and circumstance. It is really doing what Paul told us to do in Romans 12:1-2:

> *I beseech you therefore, brethren, by the mercies of God, that you present your bodies a living sacrifice, holy, acceptable to God, which is your reasonable service. And do not be conformed to this world, but be transformed by the renewing of your mind, that you may prove what is that good and acceptable and perfect will of God.*

PROSPERITY THOUGHT

Fasting is the most powerful spiritual discipline of all the Christian disciplines. Through fasting and prayer, the Holy Spirit can transform your life.

—BILL BRIGHT

Day Five

FELLOWSHIP

Let's see how inventive we can be in encouraging love and helping out, not avoiding worshiping together as some do but spurring each other on, especially as we see the big Day approaching (Hebrews 10:25 MSG).

A little wave was bobbing along in the ocean, having a grand old time. He was enjoying the wind and the fresh air—until he notices the other waves in front of him crashing against the shore. "My God, this is terrible," the wave thought. "Look what's going to happen to me!" Then along came another wave. Seeing the first wave in a panic and looking grim, it asked, "Why do you look so sad?" The first wave responded, "We're all going to crash! All of us waves are going to be nothing! Isn't this terrible?" The second wave replied with a laugh, "No, you don't understand. You will never be 'nothing,' even if you crash. Now you are only a wave, but if you crash, then you'll be part of the ocean."

When Peter announced he recognized that Jesus was *"the Christ, the Son of the living God,"*[1] Jesus responded by saying:

> *Blessed are you, Simon Bar-Jonah, for flesh and blood has not revealed this to you, but My Father who is in heaven. And I also say to you that you are Peter, and on this rock I will build My church, and the gates of Hades shall not prevail against it* (Matthew 16:17-18).

This is the first mention of the concept of church in Scripture. Jesus was saying that it would be built on the revelation of who He was. His disciples would constitute the first church members who would be His "called out ones"—called out to be part of an ocean of believers. It is the congregation of those God has "called out" of a world characterized by darkness—lacking the revelation of who God really is and the liberating truth of the gospel of Jesus Christ. To be in the world is to be separated from the message that gives meaning, purpose, dignity, and hope. As long as you are part of the Church, you are more than just a lone wave; you are part of a larger and vastly powerful sea of individuals called the family of God.

You are not on a solitary journey. It is not just that we need each other, though that is unmistakably true; it is that we are part of one another. It is somewhat like one foot trying to go on a walk without the other; an ear trying to hear for itself without the brain; an eye deceived into believing that with enough faith it can smell; a kidney thinking it can survive without the heart. As Paul so eloquently wrote to the Corinthians:

> *The human body has many parts, but the many parts make up one whole body. So it is with the body of Christ. ...If one part suffers, all the parts suffer with it, and if one part is honored, all the parts are glad. All of you together are Christ's body, and each of you is a part of it* (1 Corinthians 12:12,26-27 NLT).

And then in his letter to the Romans, Paul wrote:

> *For as we have many members in one body, but all the members do not have the same function, so we, being many, are one body in Christ, and individually members of one another. Having then gifts differing according to the grace that is given to us, let us use them* (Romans 12:4-6).

In the book of Ephesians, Paul goes so far as to call the Church, *"the fellowship of the mystery,"*[2] implying, like the beloved story, *The Fellowship of the Ring,* that we have been brought together for a mission greater than we can accomplish on our own. Not only are we together in accomplishing God's mission for the earth, but we are part of each other's mission as well. Chances are there is some key knowledge, ability, or relationship that someone in your immediate group of believers holds that could make all the difference in your walk or dreams—and there is knowledge, wisdom, skill, or ability that you hold that could be critical to what God has called them to accomplish as well.

In his book, *Where Good Ideas Come From: The Natural History of Innovation,* Steven Johnson discussed the effects of community on invention. As cities formed in early human history and people interacted more, the number of revolutionary innovations skyrocketed. The reason, he believed, was that there are a lot of people who wander around with, as it were, "part of a great solution" to some problem they had recognized. As one person with a partial idea was more likely to interact with larger numbers of people in community, it became increasingly likely that they would find a person who had, literally, the other part or parts to his or her idea. As the two or more shared their thoughts, innovation happened naturally.

> *"Just as we are not complete unto ourselves without a connection to God, neither are we complete without each other."*

In the same way, we each hold a part of the mystery of God's purposes and will for the earth. He planted it within us from before the day we were born, as He did with Jeremiah:

> *Before I shaped you in the womb, I knew all about you. Before you saw the light of day, I had holy plans for you* (Jeremiah 1:5 MSG).

Just as we are not complete unto ourselves without a connection to God, neither are we complete without each other. It is, to use the analogy of innovation, as if we were partial ideas that needed to find one another to be complete.

Thus the local church should be more than a place to gather for services. After all, the Church is not a building, but the assembly of people who meet within that building. As such, the local church is simply a designated place for the actual Church—the Body of Christ—to gather and interact, to work together so that we can find what we need to establish God's Kingdom upon the earth. The local church is an equipping and refueling place. The real work of the Church only takes place as we leave that building and go out to be our authentic selves fulfilling God's mission and extending the benefits of our knowing God to those who, as of yet, might not.

True fellowship is more than greeting and hugging each other on Sunday mornings. If we are to be the Body of Christ on the earth, then we must find ways to connect more deeply and pull from one another the gifts and callings that God has buried within each of our hearts. If we are the "mystery bearers" as Paul refers, then there are riddles to be solved and innovations to be revealed. We are called to be overcomers, but I don't believe God meant that only in regard to the issues of our individual lives. He meant it for the ills in our communities, the political disparity within your nations, the social injustices that exploit men, women, and children, and the lack that traps far too many in cycles of poverty and hunger.

Prosperity Point

Within God's mysteries are the answers our world needs. If we are to meet those needs, we have to plumb the depths of God together and dig out those solutions. We must be a church that goes out as the Church, not just as a people who gather together in a building with a steeple every Sunday to sing songs and hear a good sermon. Are we equipping each other to fulfill God's calling in our communities and the wider world? Are we meeting together hungry to discover the next piece of the puzzle of God's master plan for our lives? Or are we missing the opportunity of really being what God wants us—*the Church*—to be?

Prosperity Thought

We should no longer be children, tossed to and fro and carried about with every wind of doctrine, by the trickery of men, in the cunning craftiness of deceitful plotting, but, speaking the truth in love, may grow up in all things into Him who is the head—Christ—from whom the whole body, joined and knit together by what every joint supplies, according to the effective working by which every part does its share, causes growth of the body for the edifying of itself in love (Ephesians 4:14-16).

Week Two

INTELLECTUAL PROSPERITY

A man's mind may be likened to a garden, which may be intelligently cultivated or allowed to run wild; but whether cultivated or neglected, it must, and will, bring forth. If no useful seeds are put into it, then an abundance of useless weed seeds will fall therein, and will continue to produce their kind.

—JAMES ALLEN,
As a Man Thinketh

Day Six

READING

Five years from now, you're the same person except for the people you've met and the books you've read.
—John Wooden

I have traveled the world over, dined with emperors, fought with armies, climbed the tallest mountains, and crossed the widest oceans just by reading. As Charles Spurgeon said:

> My books are my tools. They also serve as my counsel, my consolation, and my comfort. They are my source of wisdom and the font of my education. They are my friends and my delights. They are my surety, when all else is awry, that I have set my confidence in the substantial things of truth and right.

Former U.S. President Harry Truman said it this way, "Not all readers are leaders, but all leaders are readers." I wholeheartedly agree. While there are a lot of good things to learn on television, I have found I get far more intellectual stimulation from the books I read rather than the TV programing, DVD teaching, or Internet videos I watch. More than almost any other activity, reading takes us to places we will never go on our own, challenges us to see the world through different eyes, primes our imaginations, gives us new insights and understanding into new knowledge, historical and intercultural perspectives, and opens us up to experiences we might never live ourselves. Research is finding that reading not only informs and educates us, but actually makes us better human beings.

Jim Rohn said, "Everything you need for your better future and success has already been written." He further stated, "Formal education will make you a living, self-education will make you a fortune."

World-class performers and achievers are learning machines. They understand that their investment in self-education will yield a high return. They invest heavily in books, tapes, and audio programs on subjects that are industry-specific and focus on personal and professional growth and development, leadership, management, etc. They read and study the biographies of great innovators and industry leaders attempting to extrapolate principles that they can apply to their own lives. They are always in search of better practices, keys to success, tools for improving performance, and the latest insights from world-class experts.

"Research is finding that reading not only informs and educates us, but actually makes us better human beings."

Nourish your mind (and feed your potential) by reading quality material. Like the body, it cannot work at its optimum by consuming junk. Invest in your future by investing in books. The top 1 percent of the world invests $10,000 annually on books and other learning resources that include seminars, workshops, retreats, coaching opportunities, etc. The average person may think this is a waste of time and money—many spend less annually on books than coffee. Some are more inclined to spend their money on lottery tickets, TV programming, designer bags (or shoes!), movie tickets, or fast food than on quality information and education. Make a commitment to become a lifelong learner!

Reading is also being shown to improve how we relate to and connect with others. A recent study discussed in *Scientific American Mind, Forbes, Harvard Business Review,* and other magazines suggests that by diving into the minds of characters in novels, we find a way to better empathize with and understand others. By observing the world from perspectives other than our own, we are able to grow as well as build greater capacity for tolerance and respect. We gain a greater social and cultural proficiency, which allows for cross-cultural collaboration and the subsequent progress of humanity through shared perspectives, information, and innovation.

When ninety-four individuals were asked to determine the emotions of different pictures of eyes, researchers discovered that "The more fiction people [had] read, the better they were at perceiving emotion in the eyes, and...correctly interpreting social cues."[1] In many ways, reading about a character is like running a computer simulation—we get to "try out" different things in an abstract world without complications spilling over into the real world. The researchers likened it to pilots training on flight simulators. The more time pilots spend on simulators, the better they are as pilots for real planes. In a similar way, the more we read—the more we "simulate" human interactions by exploring different scenarios, feelings, and motives through fictional characters—the better we become at flying our own lives. As Oscar Wilde is credited with saying, "It is what you read when you don't have to that determines what you will be when you can't help it."

While I enjoy reading books by great philosophers and thinkers, spiritual teachers, leadership gurus, and success experts, I find that reading about history and biography is most important to my own growth. I am fascinated to learn about the lives of people I admire and the events that shaped us into the people we are and the world in which we live. Aside from meeting some of these accomplished people face to face, reading about their lives is the best way to get to know them, especially autobiographers, who wrote their stories themselves.

There is no better way outside of meeting Him in prayer, for example, to get to know Jesus than to read the four Gospels written by Matthew, Mark, Luke, and John. However, had He written

His own autobiography, you can be sure I would have read it and gotten copies for all of my friends and family.

Books have the ability to take us into great minds and pivotal times. They let us explore the decisions that were made, the mistakes, the triumphs, and the defeats, as well as the principles that were learned and lived. They allow us to explore beyond the boundaries of what is accepted as possible and ask, "Why not?" Books allow us to learn from the mistakes of others without us having to make those same mistakes ourselves. We can get insight into the personalities and humanity of great men and women of God, industry, politics, innovation, humanitarianism, and whatever other field perks our interest. As author George R.R. Martin put it, "A reader lives a thousand lives before he dies. The man who never reads lives only one."

> *"Few other activities will prosper your mind as much as reading broadly and persistently."*

There is wealth in books of all kinds, because the love of learning is a key element of prosperity. In the same way that there is a high correlation between material success and goal setting, there is also a crucial connection between reading and prospering financially. As Zig Ziglar once described it, "Rich people have small TVs and big libraries, and poor people have small libraries and big TVs." There are just so many things that correlate between people who read a great deal and those who prosper.

In addition to these benefits, reading aids our communication skills, especially for those who are writers. Very few good writers aren't great readers—in fact, I have never met a writer who doesn't have a pile of books on his or her desk or bedside table. Reading informs living, and living informs writing. It is a natural process.

Reading will increase your vocabulary and give you new ways to communicate ideas. This helps me in both my writing and speaking. You can survive as a communicator for a while without reading, but I have found that your ideas dry up and you can feel like you are saying the same thing over and over again. You've got to keep stretching your mind and growing with reading. The best way to prosper your mind is to start learning any new thing by pulling a stack of books from the library shelf and digging in.

Prosperity Point

You should get used to having at least two books with you in your travel bag at all times: Your Bible and whatever you are currently reading. Limit, if not eliminate, your TV watching and replace it with reading at least an hour or two a day. Ask God what you should be reading for personal development and for pleasure—and dive in! Few other activities will prosper your mind as much as reading broadly and persistently.

Prosperity Thought

Read not to contradict and confute; nor to believe and take for granted; nor to find talk and discourse; but to weigh and consider. Some books are to be tasted, others to be swallowed, and some few to be chewed and digested; that is, some books are to be read only in parts; others to be read, but not curiously; and some few to be read wholly, and with diligence and attention.

—Francis Bacon,
The Essays

Day Seven

FOCUS

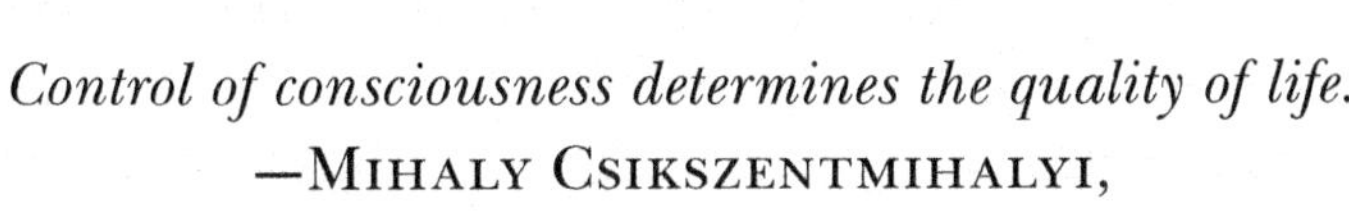

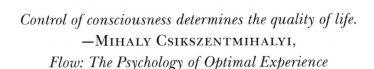

Control of consciousness determines the quality of life.
—Mihaly Csikszentmihalyi,
Flow: The Psychology of Optimal Experience

Have you ever wished you had just one or two more hours in a day to complete certain things—or at the very least to compensate for what seems like perpetual sleep deprivation? There are days in my schedule when I simply don't know where the time goes—or wonder, "Who has time to sleep?" No matter who you are, you get the same twenty-four hours each day as everyone else. So how is it that some people manage to do so much more, including sleep, no matter how busy they are, than the rest of us? In fact, I've often heard it said, "If you want something done, give it to a busy person!"

Focus.

Focus will help you manage the tyranny of the urgent. Focus will keep your life from spinning out of control. A research study was done on what separates individuals who win the Olympic gold medal, a prestigious marathon, or national championship, from other athletes who have as much talent but never obtain the prize. The scientists found it was the athletes' ability to stay focused under stress that made the difference. Focus? Not talent? Yes, focus.

The number one thing that will keep you from achieving any goal is lack of focus. Renowned author and speaker, Nido Qubein, said, "Nothing can add more power to your life than concentrating all your energies on a limited set of targets." Focus is sustained concentration of thought and action to the exclusion of other thoughts and actions. Wherever you place your focus, the rest of your mind, talents, abilities, and emotions will follow. World-class champions and performers are individuals who with relentless focus accomplish incredible feats. Their focus creates such an intense level of commitment that sparks seem to fly when they engage their entire being in the achievement of a goal.

Distraction is the bane of creativity. To plumb deeper lines of thinking, we need deeper and longer periods of concentration—something that seems increasingly difficult in today's society. Opportunities to focus are more precious than ever. I remember the day when people used to carry pagers that would vibrate and let them know they needed to call someone back, and people used to comment on how disruptive the devices were. Today, we carry smart phones that not only vibrate for phone calls, but also for emails, tweets, alarm reminders, and whenever a friend updates their social media status. And not only that, we are tempted to check them constantly to make sure we're not missing something. It's gotten to the point that it's difficult to spend a mere half hour in a meeting or conversation without a phone going off.

Furthermore, if you're someone like me who will frequently pull out the phone to record a new idea, or check messages, you risk undermining your ability to focus. And that's only your phone! Add to that your other screens and devices, your kids, your boss, your spouse, your friends, your pets, or whatever else demands your attention—and it's a wonder you ever get anything done!

The sad truth is, a lot of us don't.

Our modern society seems wired to make us jacks-of-all-trades and masters of none. "Multitasking" is the order of the day, requiring us to pay attention to a lot of different things with only portions of ourselves. For smaller tasks like clicking through junk email, scrolling through Facebook posts and Twitter feeds, or clearing our desks of clutter, being able to multitask can be a good thing, but it can also be a habit that draws us away from the really important things in life, like listening intently when we are with others, reading, thinking, creating, or praying. Along with the ability to check off multiple items on our to-do lists, we must also cultivate the ability to slow down, be still, and be fully present in any one moment in order to focus deeply on *one thing*.

The most beneficial state is what author and researcher Mihaly Csikszentmihalyi calls "flow." Many in the sports world call this "being in the zone." It's that state of complete concentration and focus that shuts out the roaring crowd, sees the "game" in its essential elements, and recognizes the path to victory with laser-like focus.

In the film *For the Love of the Game,* Kevin Costner is an aging pitcher threatened with either being traded or pushed into retirement. He has one last game to prove his worth. Each time he takes the mound, he goes through a little routine to focus his mind telling himself to "clear the mechanism." As he says this, the crowd noise muffles, the baseball diamond around him disappears, and suddenly all he sees is the lane between himself and the catcher behind the plate. The entire game of baseball breaks down to roughly a hundred little games of a single pitch. As he does this inning after inning, pitch after pitch, he finds himself oblivious to the fact that he hasn't allowed a runner or hit through eight innings. As he goes out for the ninth, on the verge of pitching a perfect game, that focus begins to waver, and the drama of the film comes to its height: *Can he find that place of composed concentration for just a few more pitches and complete his perfect game?*

> *"Most successful people don't do a dozen little things well, but find one true calling, cut away the distractions, and pour their hearts into doing that one thing better than anyone else."*

The Bible tells us, "*Whatever you do, do your work heartily, as for the Lord rather than for men.*"[1] To me, that speaks of a focus that takes each activity of our day—as we pass through each realm of life, working to prosper spiritually, intellectually, emotionally, physically, in our relationships, in society, vocationally, and financially—and giving ourselves wholeheartedly to whatever we are doing in the moment. We don't take our jobs home with us to siphon attention away from our families, we don't allow an argument with our boss to affect how we treat others, and we plan our weekly and daily schedules to prioritize the important things. We find ways of clearing our physical, emotional, and intellectual spaces for chunks of time that will allow us to focus on what is most important in that moment—things that prosper our relationships, our reputation, our careers, and our finances. We learn to take time aside from the noise of life, carve out blocks of solitude, hear from Heaven, and birth into the world the contribution we were created to make.

Most successful people don't do a dozen little things well, but find one true calling, cut away the distractions, and pour their hearts into doing that one thing better than anyone else in the world. Even if they are involved in very complicated endeavors, they find a way of breaking it down into bite-sized goals and making each part simple. They focus on just one bite before moving to the next. Denis Waitley once said, "Goals provide the energy source that powers our lives. One of the best ways we can get the most from the energy we have is to focus it." This is why the power of focus is such an important skill in learning to prosper your soul and living the life God has for you.

Whatever you focus on today, you give permission to exist tomorrow. Focus on your dreams, goals, and future. Focus on where you want to be, not where you are. Focus on what you hope to have and what you wish to do—not on what you do not have or have not done. Focus on your healing and not your sickness. Focus on your deliverance and not your detrimental situation. Focus on what remains and not what you have lost—or the weight you hope to lose and not what you've gained! Dream about how different your life can be, then wake up and focus on making it happen so that you can live the life of your dreams.

Prosperity Point

You are not a victim of circumstances, but the creator of your future. "One of the fundamental differences between the victim-orientation and [the creator]," said David Emerald, "is where you put your focus:"

> For victims, the focus is always on what they don't want: The problems that seem constantly to multiply in their lives. They don't want the person, condition, or circumstance they consider their persecutor, and they don't want the fear that leads to fight, flee, or freeze reactions, either. Creators, on the other hand, place their focus on what they do want. Doing this, creators still face and solve problems in the course of creating outcomes they want, but their focus remains fixed on their ultimate vision.[2]

We must not let the tyranny of the urgent steal away from what is important and foundational. When you focus on creating the outcome you desire, you will not only find that place of "flow"—that creative abandon and joy of fully living into all you are called to be—but you will grow and prosper in ways you never imagined possible.

Prosperity Thought

Always remember,
your focus determines your reality.
—George Lucas

Day Eight

CREATIVITY

Imagination is everything. It is the preview of life's coming attractions.
—ALBERT EINSTEIN

There is an old saying, "Necessity is the mother of invention," but I don't believe that is true. At best, "Necessity is the father of invention," because it gives the seed that leads to invention. It is *imagination* that is the mother of invention, for it is in the imagination that the seed is received, the idea is conceived, and where experimentation is analyzed, refined, and perfected. Needs, after all, are all around us. What is necessary is that more creative people take those needs into their imaginations, gestate them, and come up with problem-solving innovations.

Let me give you an example. I recently saw a YouTube video entitled "The Science of Fiction" by Robert Wong. Robert is a graphic designer who was part of the team that started Google Creative Lab. He is not an inventor or technician, but when he and his team were shown some of the work that was being done on creating glasses that utilized smart phone technology, his team decided to make a commercial for the product before they even knew what it would be. They didn't base it on what it currently could do, but what might be possible. At that point, no one knew how Google glasses would actually work—the technicians were too occupied with issues of size, weight, comfort, projection, computing power, etc. They weren't yet pondering about the possibilities of the technology; they were focused solely on its limitations.

So in stepped the team from the Creative Lab. With no limitations except their own imaginations, the team created a commercial for the product based on what they thought would be cool. When they showed it to the engineers, the engineers were awed. They said, "Let's make that!" Others joked, "Maybe you should make a film like this every week!" The team was inspired in whole new ways, and as I am writing this, prototypes of the Google Glass[1] are already being released for experimentation to "explorers" across the United States.

Mr. Wong goes on to point out that science fiction has often influenced real-world technology. He notes that Martin Cooper at Motorola, one of the inventers of the cellular phone, was a huge "Star Trek" fan (remember the handheld communicators they flipped open all the time? How much do cell phones look like that today?). He also noted a Twitter exchange between Elon Musk, CEO of Tesla Motors and Space X, and Jon Favreau, the director of *Iron Man*. Musk said, "We figured out how to design rocket parts with just hand gestures through the air (seriously)." Favreau tweeted to him, "Like in *Iron Man?*" Musk tweeted back, "Yup. We saw it in the movie and made it real. Good idea!"

"*You never know the true value of an idea until it's connected with the right knowledge.*"

Some of us think that just because we are not technological geniuses like Elon Musk, we won't influence the future or contribute to innovation, but you never know the true value of an idea until it's connected with the right knowledge. The world needs people who are obsessed with pursuing God and His witty inventions in order to solve real-world problems. Life is your creative laboratory. Never underestimate the power of a need, an idea, and some ingenuity to find one another and combust into a game-changing innovation.

But then you may say, "But I'm not creative. What does that have to do with me?" Mark Bryan, Julia Cameron, and Catherine Allen, the authors of *The Artist's Way at Work,* wrote in their introduction, "Creativity is not limited to a select few. It is a universal, not an elitist, gift. Creativity belongs, as a birthright, to all of us."[2]

> *You can discover keys to amazing breakthroughs simply by seeing things a little differently—by doing things that help you connect the dots in new ways.*

If you can imagine, you can create. If you can dream, you can make a difference.

We all tend to underestimate the importance of our ideas or the power of our own discernment. We may think we are not smart enough, not imaginative enough, not technically educated enough, or just not important enough, but it doesn't always work that way. In the Bible, there is a story about a city that was under siege, and the answer for its salvation came from an unimportant pauper who was soon forgotten:

> *There was a little city with few men in it; and a great king came against it, besieged it, and built great snares around it. Now there was found in it a poor wise man, and he by his wisdom delivered the city. ...Then I said: "Wisdom is better than strength"* (Ecclesiastes 9:14-16).

Even though no one remembered his name, this man saved every member of his town from a great army. And you can be sure that even if the townspeople forgot this man, God never did.

You are a change agent, a powerful voice, a difference maker...even if only for those whose lives you touch in your immediate vicinity. No one sees things like you do. No one shares your set of experiences, background, and "ahas" you've encountered. No one has exactly the same gifts you have. No one can connect the dots just like you can. God created you for a specific reason, and His world is not complete without what He designed you to contribute to it. Never underestimate the power and importance of your own creativity. Cherish and develop it every day.

Prosperity Point

The key to transformation for a company, an organization, a church, a family, or even your own life can come from anywhere. You might read it in a book, you might see it in a film, you might hear it in prayer, you might discover it while scribbling in your journal. You must develop your creativity by paying attention to the world around you. Look for needs—and then provide solutions. When Margaret Rudkin, a forty-year-old mother of three, created a whole wheat bread recipe for her son who had severe allergies, Pepperidge Farm was born. She ran the company for more than twenty years before selling it to Campbell Soup in 1961.[3]

"Creativity is just connecting things," said Steve Jobs. "When you ask creative people how they did something, they feel a little guilty because they didn't really do it, they just saw something. It seemed obvious to them after a while."[4] You can discover keys to amazing breakthroughs simply by seeing things a little differently—by doing things that help you connect the dots in new ways. Embrace creativity as part of your daily process—practicing and enhancing it however your heart is led. Play music, paint pictures, journal and write, craft, bake, cook, experiment, tinker, and take time to just let yourself imagine possibilities. If you let Him, the Spirit of God will lead you into incredible and marvelous things. He has manifold mysteries He wants to share and help you unravel.

Prosperity Thought

Imagination is the beginning of creation. You imagine what you desire, you will what you imagine, and at last, you create what you will.

—George Bernard Shaw

Day Nine

STUDY

Dig deep. Find your way to your soul.
—KAMI GARCIA

Study is essential to learning. In order to learn you must become a student. You must learn the art of studying. Studying is not about the accumulation of facts, but about building capacity. As you build your capacity to do and become more, you will find yourself rising to positions of leadership—as a leader in your field, in your company, your church, or your community. Former U.S. President John F. Kennedy said, "Leadership and learning are indispensable to each other."

Without learning, there is no growth; without learning deeply, the knowledge we gain will never flourish. Learning is not just about "book knowledge." It is about life lessons—learning from your mistakes and honoring the potential for greatness that God has placed inside of you. You must cooperate with the process of honing your skills—for this will transform you and propel you to a place of greater influence.

Don't be afraid to explore new topics. When you plant a new topic in your mind, you often have the same experience with understanding as Jesus described in the parable of the sower. If you watch a video, documentary, or read about something casually in an article that peaks your interest, you will hang on to a few things about the topic—but if you apply yourself to see beyond the surface and begin to dig into it, roots of knowledge will start to sink deeply into your mind. You will see things through new intellectual lenses and understand things with more breadth and depth. This knowledge then forms a foundation for who you are becoming and what you can potentially do. The cumulative effect of digging into topics with sincere curiosity and wonder changes how you process information and what you are able to do with it. Such people become the "go-to" people; they are the experts; they are the catalysts of innovation. Focused study leads to expertise.

Things we dedicate our lives to knowing and understanding lead to what *New York Times* best-selling author Malcolm Gladwell calls the element of *Blink!* This is when the knowledge we've acquired becomes so ingrained within the way we interact with and see the world that we can look at something and know in a blink what to do about it. Within seconds of seeing something, we discern the true from the false; the truth from the lie.

"The cumulative effect of digging into topics with sincere curiosity and wonder changes how you process information and what you are able to do with it."

For me, this has happened in different ways. First of all, it has meant becoming a student of the Bible with my whole heart. It means exploring *Strong's Concordance* and *Vine's Expository Dictionary* to look up words in the original languages to see what additional insights I might glean. It means looking for other places in the Bible where that word was used and comparing the contexts. It also means looking into the people and groups to whom these Scriptures were written or spoken, investigating the culture and social norms of the times, as well as trying to understand what I am studying in relationship to the other books of the Bible where God breathed that word into the author's mind. I'm also interested to learn about that author, and if possible, where he was in his life as he penned or dictated his texts. I have been amazed at how much revelation God can lock up in a single word. The word often seems to explode with new meaning once I dig into it, looking to release what God has stored there.

I also apply myself to follow my curiosities and plumb the depths of the questions that come to my mind. In this way, God has led me to powerful new insights about success, leadership, innovation, transformation, investments, health, and a host of other subjects that have contributed to what I teach from the pulpit and what I put into my books. These questions have added intentionality to my reading and Internet browsing, helping the roots of my understanding dig deeply into the soil so that I can be more fruitful in everything I do. I study so that my teaching can touch lives and nurture others to grow deeper roots and to produce fruit of their own.

> *How wholeheartedly we apply ourselves to study the interests, curiosities, and wonderings that God plants into our hearts has a great deal to do with how fully our destinies will be realized.*

Certainly, as in school, we study to pass tests. Many times, what we have learned over the years will aid us tremendously in facing challenges at work, in life, and in relationships. It's not really about just knowing a great deal about a bunch of different things, but studying that which is of most interest to you—that will help you solve a dilemma you are facing, or make you more efficient at something you like or need to do. It's about unraveling a ball of yarn—or peeling the onion, if you will—that God has put into your soul. It is following the trail of bread crumbs He has laid out that leads to your real passion and the reason He put you on the earth. It is what you are wired for, and where your greatest happiness and satisfaction lie.

However, too many of us are like King Joash when Elisha challenged him to take his arrows and strike the ground in response to God's promise of deliverance for his nation.[1] Elisha wanted a passionate, deep response, but instead Joash seemed to just paw at the dirt, striking the ground three times. Elisha told him, *"You should have struck five or six times; then you would have struck Syria till you had destroyed it! But now you will strike Syria only three times.*"[2] God made Joash a promise, put a plan into his hands, but rather than responding enthusiastically to what God wanted him to do, Joash replied halfheartedly. He could have had complete victory over those who threatened him and protected the land of Israel forever from the enemy he faced; but instead, because of his lackluster response, Syria was only pushed back for a time. A generation or so later, they would be back to threaten Judah and Israel again.

In the same way, our destinies do not just happen because God declared them. We have to respond. Strike the ground hard. We have to dig deeply into them. How wholeheartedly we apply ourselves to study the interests, curiosities, and wonderings that God plants into our hearts has a great deal to do with how fully our destinies will be realized. Do you fully unwrap the gifts God has put into your soul? Or do you get distracted by the *"worries of this life, the lure of wealth, and the desire for other things"*[3] that derail so many and keep them from ever fully becoming who God created them to be?

Prosperity Point

There are things you need to know to fulfill your calling on the earth, and the key to unlocking them is to learn to dig deeply into what interests you, what you need to know for school or work, and the questions that seize your heart. If something doesn't interest you, but you have to learn it for some reason, use it as an exercise to learn about how you learn best, what motivates you, and how to discipline yourself to do what needs to be done. Never let distractions keep you from prospering in whatever you set your hand to do or learn. Whatever you do, do it with all your heart as unto God—even your studies—and you will reap the rewards of all He has planned for you.

Prosperity Thought

Until you know that life is interesting—and find it so—you haven't found your soul.

—Geoffrey Fisher

Day Ten

WISDOM

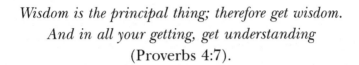

Wisdom is the principal thing; therefore get wisdom. And in all your getting, get understanding (Proverbs 4:7).

Wisdom is more than knowing things. To know or understand something is to have facts, figures, and information at your fingertips. To be wise, however, is something different—it is the ability to apply that knowledge in any given situation so that your knowledge makes a positive difference. As a minister friend of mine once said when asked about how to succeed, he replied, "Just make all the right decisions." To make the right decisions, you have to be knowledgeable about your options, yet you need wisdom to discern the best among those choices. As the saying goes, "Knowledge is knowing a tomato is a fruit; wisdom is not putting it in a fruit salad."

In the Bible we are told that Solomon, the writer of the books of Proverbs, Ecclesiastes, and the Song of Solomon, was one of the wisest men who ever lived, perhaps wiser than any person who ever walked the earth aside from Jesus. We know that God appeared to him in a dream not long after he became king and made him an offer he couldn't refuse: *"Ask! What shall I give you?"*[1] Rather than riches, a great kingdom, fame, a long life, or victory in battle, Solomon asked for wisdom so that he could justly rule the people of God. God was pleased and told him what a great decision he had made:

> *Behold, I have done according to your words; see, I have given you a wise and understanding heart, so that there has not been anyone like you before you, nor shall any like you arise after you. And I have also given you what you have not asked: Both riches and honor, so that there shall not be anyone like you among the kings all your days. So if you walk in My ways, to keep My statutes and My commandments, as your father David walked, then I will lengthen your days* (1 Kings 3:12-14).

Soon after this dream, Solomon was confronted by two prostitutes who each claimed a certain infant as her own. Both had given birth about the same time, and while the two slept in a house together alone, one of them (probably in a drunken stupor) rolled over on her infant and suffocated it. Waking up and finding her child dead, she switched him with the child of her housemate, or so said the other woman. Now both came before Solomon saying the living child was her own.

Solomon weighed their testimony carefully, and in a stroke of insight commanded, *"Divide the living child in two, and give half to one, and half to the other."*[2] The mother who'd spoken truthfully cried out, *"O my lord, give her the living child, and by no means kill him!"* While the other spat out, *"Let him be neither mine nor yours, but divide him."*[3] Noting the first had the compassion of a true mother, Solomon commanded, *"Give the first woman the living child, and by no means kill him; she is his mother."*[4]

Such wisdom is uncanny on so many levels. Solomon literally looked into the eyes of these two women and came up with a test that would reveal the nature of their hearts for all to see. His knowledge of human nature was not enough; he also needed divine insight into the facts he had before him so that he could discern a test to reveal the truth. Once he acted in wisdom, the best course of action for this child's future became plain.

The Bible also tells us:

The fear of the Lord is the beginning of wisdom, and the knowledge of the Holy One is understanding (Proverbs 9:10).

The "fear of the Lord" is not a very politically correct concept in our day and age. We hear a lot about God as a loving Father—which He truly is—but not so much about the awesomeness of His full presence or the trepidation we should have about making anything a priority before Him. To fear God, however, is not to be shaking in our shoes that we might do something wrong because that might cause Him to rain down hail and brimstone upon us. We do not live in an age of judgment, but an age of grace. What we should fear, however, is trying to live without Him at the center of our lives. If He is at the center, how could we possibly make any major decision without consulting Him or considering His precepts? To fear God is to put nothing before Him out of dread that we might miss out on His best for us.

"To fear God is to put nothing before Him out of dread that we might miss out on His best for us."

To fear—many prefer the word *reverence*—is to always think of Him first in any situation. To revere Him is to put pleasing Him before anything else—before our own opinions, our own desires, our own dreams, and what we think is for our best. To "fear" God in this way, then, is to fear nothing else—not failure, not "missing out," not what others think, not what others might do, not anything other than pleasing Him. To fear God is to recognize how foolhardy it is to look to anyone or anything else. In the New Testament, Jesus clarifies this concept for us, saying that if we *"seek first the kingdom of God and His righteousness, and all these things* [He was speaking of material provision at the time] *shall be added to you."*[5] To "fear" God is to reverence God, holding Him first in all things, and to be smart enough not to let anything ever displace the desire to please Him in every action we take.

Solomon's wisdom came from God. When he thought of God first in everything he did and refused to make a decision or take an action without seeking Him first and honoring Him, Israel prospered. However, later in his life when his womanizing tied his heart to his many wives and concubines instead of God, things changed for him dramatically. The great promise of what Israel could do faded, and God eventually had to wrestle the leadership of Israel away from Solomon's heirs because they rejected putting God first in everything. Selfish ambition poisoned them and they turned their back on wisdom. This proves that wisdom is also a choice; it is not enough to know the right thing to do, you must choose to do it.

> *"Wisdom starts when you allow God to work His good through you no matter what you face."*

God wants to freely grant us wisdom, just as He granted Solomon after his prayer. The apostle James advised, *"If any of you lacks wisdom, let him ask of God, who gives to all liberally and without reproach, and it will be given to him."*[6] As we seek God and multiply what we know in the natural through prospering our intellects, God will connect the dots of our understanding. He will give us the insights we need to realize the breakthroughs we are pursuing.

The wisdom of God comes as we steadfastly follow Him, listen for His voice, and obey what we hear. When we let His principles inform our decision making and allow Him to show us the way He sees things, wisdom comes in ways we would never expect.

Prosperity Point

Albert Einstein said, "Wisdom is not a product of schooling, but of the lifelong attempt to acquire it." It is not learning so much as seeing things as God sees them, letting Him give us His insights, and then acting accordingly. To be wise is to know what to do in the circumstances we face. It is built on knowledge and understanding, as God breathes His insights into our minds.

Wisdom starts when you allow God to work His good through you no matter what you face. After a repeat DWI offender killed her thirteen-year-old daughter, Candy Lightner founded Mothers Against Drunk Driving (MADD) in her home on March 7, 1980. Before MADD, there were little to no legal consequences for driving while intoxicated; her organization transformed American attitudes about drunk driving and successfully fought for stricter laws across the country.[7] Her daughter's death changed her world, but through the wisdom of God, she changed ours.

Be open to that and seek it with all your heart, for *"He who gets wisdom loves his own soul; He who keeps understanding will find good."*[8]

Prosperity Thought

It's not hard to make decisions when
you know what your values are.
—Roy Disney

Week Three

EMOTIONAL PROSPERITY

Guard your heart above all else, for it determines the course of your life (Proverbs 4:23 NLT).

Day Eleven

JOY

Be energetic in your life of salvation, reverent and sensitive before God. That energy is God's energy, an energy deep within you, God himself willing and working at what will give him the most pleasure (Philippians 2:13 MSG).

There is nothing more tragic than to be alive and not have joy. The joy of the Lord is your strength—it is a powerful medicine and an overcoming spiritual force.

Joy is not an emotion, but an attitude—a state of mind or manner of being. Isaiah 61:3 talks about putting on the oil of joy and a garment of praise like you would a healing salve or a protective cloak. Joy is to be applied and worn. It is putting on an attitude of gratitude no matter the situation or circumstance. You cannot be grateful while at the same time overcome by feelings of remorse—when gratitude wells up in your heart, so does joy; nor can you be joyful while at the same time overwhelmed by self-pity and bitterness—joy will give rise to gratitude. Joy, gratitude, and praise are very much intertwined.

Joy can cause the world to look like a different place. Quite often it is not so much something that bursts forth from the inside of us as it is a choice we make—and sometimes it is a choice we must fight for. As Paulo Coelho wrote, "Joy is sometimes a blessing, but it is often a conquest."

Joy and prosperity go hand in hand. When you consider the impact your attitude has on your thoughts, perceptions, and actions, you will begin to nurture and groom your attitude and put it to positive use. It is a tool, a weapon, a treasure, and a contagion. Its influence affects everyone you come into contact with. It is a gift you can give in any situation. William Jones said, "The greatest discovery of any generation is that a human being can alter his life [and the lives of others] by altering his attitude."

The Bible tells us that joy is a fruit of the Spirit, second only to love.[1] The book of Proverbs tells us that joy comes from doing what is right and just, *"The exercise of justice is joy for the righteous,"*[2] and the book of Matthew tells us that those who manage God's gifts and talents well will be invited to *"enter into the joy of your lord."*[3] Jesus taught His disciples certain truths and principles, saying it was so *"My joy may remain in you, and that your joy may be full."*[4] On the night before He was to be crucified, He instructed them that once He had gone to His Father, they were to ask the Father in His name for whatever it was they desired so that *"you will receive, that your joy may be full."*[5] Paul later went so far as to proclaim that one of the key components of the Kingdom of God was *"joy in the Holy Spirit."*[6]

> *Joy is connected not with the alignment of outside circumstances so much as the continued choice of living in a certain way toward a desired end.*

But I think it was the apostle James who made it most obvious that joy is a choice:

> *My brethren, count it all joy when you fall into various trials, knowing that the testing of your faith produces patience. But let patience have its perfect work, that you may be perfect and complete, lacking nothing* (James 1:2-4).

Happiness is a state of passing tranquility; it has an element of good fortune to it, as well as an overwhelming power to keep one in the moment, worried neither about what the future may hold or the past has presented. Joy, however, is much more rarely such a happenstance. Joy is connected not with the alignment of outside circumstances so much as the continued choice of living in a certain way toward a desired end. Happiness happens to us; joy, however, comes from living for something greater than ourselves. The writer of Hebrews tells us that even Jesus aligned His steps in the hope of one day experiencing the joy of fulfilling the purpose for which He came to the earth.

> *Jesus...who for the joy that was set before Him endured the cross, despising the shame, and has sat down at the right hand of the throne of God* (Hebrews 12:2).

Thus it is, in the midst of unhappiness—in the midst of the world throwing its worst at us—as James advised, we can choose to rejoice because we are living for something greater than anything that temporary circumstances can defeat. We are living for something deeper, something more beneficial to those around us, something rooted in seeing more of the Kingdom of God manifested through our actions, decisions, and obedience to the calling of our hearts. As Tommy Newberry wrote in his best-selling book, *40 Days to a Joy-Filled Life:*

> Joy is a state of mind that must be purposely cultivated if you are to live and love and influence others as God intended. Fortunately, joy does not depend on the outer conditions of your material life, but rather on the inner conditions of your mental life. Joy is the result of something strikingly simple, though not necessarily easy: *Consistently thinking joy-producing thoughts.*[7]

In this way, joy is foundational, while happiness is window-dressing—it can make a room, but it's not going to hold up the house. Happiness is the icing, but joy is the cake. If we choose joy—if we live for it rather than mere happiness—happiness will still come on its own; but if we live instead to be happy, we often live frustrated lives because we don't always have control of the circumstances around us. Chasing happiness might also cause us to fall too easily into those things that bring temporary enjoyment but no lasting fulfillment: Over-indulging in entertainment, hiding in the temporary highs of substance abuse, shallow sexual stimulation from pornography or promiscuity, wasting our time with gossip and backbiting, getting lost in the virtual world of video games or social media, etc. Happiness from such distractions is fleeting, and at the end of it we have nothing left but the memory of a handful of pleasant experiences. Joy, however, endures. It is built on seeing substantial change made in the lives of others, experiencing an expansion of Kingdom thinking, having our paradigms shifted to see things more as God does, or knowing in our hearts that we have today made a difference that will affect someone's eternity.

Prosperity Point

To choose joy is to acknowledge the presence of God in any given situation. To experience joy, as Pierre Teilhard de Chardin put it, "is the infallible sign of the presence of God."

From joy comes boundless spiritual strength of spirit, though this is rarely a spectacular aspect. Instead, it acts as an inner engine, feeding your faith, conviction, and ability to give of yourself—your ability to do what is right. Storms of hostility, bitterness, unwarranted criticism, negativity, strife, and the like may roar toward you, but if you choose joy and refuse to let go of it—picking a bigger paradigm view than one that only sees the temporary setbacks—you will be able to overcome them, or at least outlast them. As Nehemiah recognized, *"The joy of the Lord is your strength"*[8]—and when you walk with God, choosing joy no matter what you face, you will grow into the person God is calling you to be: *"Mature and well-developed, not deficient in any way."*[9]

PROSPERITY THOUGHT

If you wish to glimpse inside a human soul and get to know a man, don't bother analyzing his ways of being silent, of talking, of weeping, of seeing how much he is moved by noble ideas; you will get better results if you just watch him laugh. If he laughs well, he's a good man.

—FYODOR DOSTOYEVSKY

Day Twelve

PEACE

These things I have spoken to you, that in Me you may have peace. In the world you will have tribulation; but be of good cheer, I have overcome the world (John 16:33).

Has anyone ever asked you something like, "What's up with you? What's going on? There's something different about you. How can you always be so calm? Doesn't anything ever get you riled?"

If not, maybe you should recalibrate how you are applying the promises of God so that they do.

One of the most common titles Paul uses in his letters to refer to God is "the God of peace," and he usually uses this title when speaking a blessing over the readers. Jesus was commonly referred to as "The Prince of Peace." In the Old Testament, the corresponding title used was *Jehovah-Shalom,* which means, "The Lord Is Peace." Notice that the title isn't "The Lord Who Gives Peace" or "The Lord Our Peace" as is the form of many of the other Old Testament titles used to reveal God's character, but it's "The Lord *Is* Peace." This means that in the same way the Scriptures tell us that *"God is love,"*[1] peace is not something God gives but is central to the very nature of who God is.

We know that God is a trinity—three in one—the Father, the Son, and the Holy Spirit. If the Triune God is *love,* then that infers that the relationship between each member of the Godhead is a bond of love that cannot be broken—so strong, in fact, that the three are actually one. If that is true, then it is also true of *peace.* The peace we experience in Christ should be one that is also defined by the relationship of the three-as-one.

Vine's Expository Dictionary defines *shalom,* the Hebrew word for "peace," as follows:

> The relationship is one of harmony and wholeness, which is the opposite of the state of strife and war. ...Shalom, as a harmonious state of the soul and mind, encourages the development of the faculties and powers. The state of being at ease is experienced both externally and internally....
>
> *Shalom* also signifies "peace," indicative of a prosperous relationship between two or more parties.

As in the Godhead, peace is expressed in relationship. It is one thing to not strive or fight, but to be at peace is much more. To be at peace is to sincerely desire to bless the other. It is not an "I'll scratch your back if you scratch mine" sort of partnership arrangement, but a deep commitment to one another according to the unconditional love of God. It comes, really, in a series of relationships:

1. Our relationship with God,
2. Our relationship with ourselves,
3. Our relationship with those closest to us,
4. Our relationship with those we interact with regularly, and
5. Our relationship with the world around us.

The Bible tells us:

> *We have peace with God because of what Jesus Christ our Lord has done for us. Because of our faith, Christ has brought*

> *us into this place of undeserved privilege where we now stand* (Romans 5:1-2 NLT).

To be at peace with God opens the door to spend time in His presence and be able to ask to perceive and experience everything from His paradigm—including how He sees us. To see ourselves as God sees us is to be at peace with who we are now and who we are becoming. This is to live with our minds set on His spiritual perspective, and *"the mind set on the Spirit is life and peace."*[2]

These two internal relationships—with God and ourselves—are shown to the world through our relationship with those who are closest to us first, and then those we interact with on a regular basis. The lack of peace in our souls is generally most visible in how we interact with whom we are closest—a parent, a child, or a spouse. If there is strife in these relationships, we need to do some serious soul searching to see how we are doing in our relationship with God and with ourselves. If there is a lack of peace in our most intimate external relationships, then there is more than likely a fundamental inner conflict as well.

"To see ourselves as God sees us is to be at peace with who we are now and who we are becoming."

A solid foundation of peace in those first three relationships determines how we reach out with peace into the world around us—both with the people we interact with regularly and the world at large. Knowing we have foundational peace also gives us the confidence to know that Heaven is open to our prayers, thus allowing us to be at peace—that overpowering, difficult-to-understand sort of peace—that brings tranquility to our relationships. As the Scriptures say:

> *Don't worry about anything; instead, pray about everything. Tell God what you need, and thank him for all he has done. Then you will experience God's peace, which exceeds anything we can understand. His peace will guard your hearts and minds as you live in Christ Jesus* (Philippians 4:6-7 NLT).

The peace of God is not only tranquil, but also courageous and assertive. It gives us a backbone to stand up for what is right, take up the cause of those who cannot stand up for themselves, as well as to do it in a nonviolent, insightful, and respectful way. Bound by love in its highest form, we are also bound by justice, mercy, and faithfulness. This means that expanding the Kingdom of God is not passive, even though it is peaceful. It knows when to say no to injustice and unrighteousness, it knows how to stand when right is on the line, but it also knows that those who oppose us are not the enemy; our battle is with the spiritual forces hoodwinking them into standing for the wrong things.

In everything we do, we are to pursue peace, for it is the umpire of our souls, helping us to divide between what seems right and what actually is. As Paul wrote to the Colossians:

> *Let the peace (soul harmony which comes) from Christ rule (act as umpire continually) in your hearts [deciding and settling with finality all questions that arise in your minds, in that peaceful state] to which as [members of Christ's] one body you were also called [to live]* (Colossians 3:15 AMP).

This peace should then ooze out into everything you do. It should be visible for others to see. It should be one of your most obvious personality traits. It is Jesus shining from the inside out of you. It is, most markedly, what makes us as Christians different from the rest of the world.

Prosperity Point

Paul urges us to pursue peace in all things, for of all the fruit of the Spirit, it makes us and marks us as representatives of God, whatever our calling may be:

> *I, therefore, the prisoner of the Lord, beseech you to walk worthy of the calling with which you were called, with all lowliness and gentleness, with longsuffering, bearing with one another in love, endeavoring to keep the unity of the Spirit in the bond of peace* (Ephesians 4:1-3).

This is the peace that comes from knowing who we are in God's eyes and who we are as His ambassadors. Embrace peace as a firm foundation upon which to prosper your soul.

Prosperity Thought

You find peace not by rearranging the circumstances of your life, but by realizing who you are at the deepest level.
—Eckhart Tolle

Day Thirteen

FORTITUDE

God is strong, and he wants you strong. So take everything the Master has set out for you, well-made weapons of the best materials. And put them to use so you will be able to stand up to everything the devil throws your way (Ephesians 6:10-11 MSG).

You hear a lot about "core strength" these days. Sports scientists have learned that it is not enough to have big biceps and strong legs, but you have to be solid and fit from within—from your core. Thus more and more athletes work as hard—if not harder—developing core strength than they do any other group of muscles in their bodies.

The same is true for our whole essence as human beings. Some exercise their bodies and judge the world according to their outer, physical senses—but doing so fails to tap into the richer world we have through knowing God and understanding the spiritual world. It's an inside-out job. Others do their best to focus on the spiritual realm, digging deeply into the things of the spirit and exercising their spiritual senses to the point, as the old saying goes, "They are so heavenly minded they are no earthly good."

However, our true core—the center of our beings—is not in the midpoint of our body; it is the soul. As we have discussed before, the soul is made up of the mind, will, and emotions. Of these, our true motivator, the core of our core if you will, is our emotions. We judge with our intellects, we act according to what our wills decide, but it is emotion that moves us. Unfortunately, sometimes it moves us in good ways and sometimes in bad.

Of the ancient cardinal virtues suggested by Saint Thomas Aquinas, *fortitude*—what we might call the "core strength" of the soul—was considered to be the perfection of emotional appetites. This did not mean, necessarily, that one was "emotionally strong," but that one had the capacity to do what was right and just, even when emotion might point us in a different direction. This fortitude is the source of courage in the face of fear, of peace when confronted with anger, and of love in response to abuse or cruelty just as Jesus instructed us:

> *You have heard that it was said, "An eye for an eye and a tooth for a tooth." But I tell you not to resist an evil person. But whoever slaps you on your right cheek, turn the other to him also* (Matthew 5:38-39).

It is the ability to harness emotion—positive or negative—as raw power and channel it as we see fit. This virtue is as often referred to as "courage" as it is "fortitude," for it is exemplified by the ability to muster a better emotion when a weaker one would keep us from doing what is right.

Such moral fortitude was exhibited in the Civil Rights Movement as well as the nonviolent protests inspired by Gandhi in India. A good example is from a story I read recently that took place on a spring afternoon of 1963 in Birmingham, Alabama.

Civil rights protests had been taking place daily for some time—and the jails were virtually overflowing with those arrested and imprisoned from these rallies. As the numbers increased, local law enforcement felt it needed to act more harshly to halt the steady flow of protesters being locked up. According to Martin Luther King Jr.'s autobiography:

> The result was an ugliness too well known to Americans and to people all over the world. The newspapers of May 4

> carried pictures of prostrate women, and policemen bending over them with raised clubs; of children marching up to the bared fangs of police dogs; of the terrible force of pressure hoses sweeping bodies into the streets.[1]

Then one Sunday afternoon several hundred protesters gathered at the New Pilgrim Baptist Church for a march to the jail where they planned to hold a prayer meeting. Just days before a similar group had been beaten and imprisoned, and despite this threat, this new group wanted to go pray with them. Hearing of the march, the local sheriff, Bull Connor, gathered his officers, police dogs, and attached fire hoses to hydrants preparing to meet them and stop them in their tracks. Officers dressed in full riot gear. They steadied, standing their ground resolutely as this group of men, women, teenagers, and children, all decked out in their Sunday best, approached from up the street.

Sherriff Connor shouted out to them that they needed to turn back.

The leader of the group, Reverend Charles Billups, politely refused.

"Turn on the hoses!" Connor shouted without even turning around.

The air hung heavy with the order, everyone there knowing full well it meant turning the full wrath of police authority on men, women, and children armed with nothing more than the Bibles many of them carried. The order hung for a tense moment. Some of the protesters knelt, clasping their hands before them as in prayer. Others stood glaring back at the officers, many of them taking the hands of the person next to them readying themselves for the deluge.

Another tense moment passed.

Then one of the protesters in the front took a step forward to continue on his way. Others followed. Those on their knees rose up to go with them.

The wall of police officers slowly stepped back to let them through. No one lifted a weapon or a hand to impede them.

Shortly afterward, the group prayed at the jail. No one was arrested. No one interfered with the group. There was no scene made. Once the meeting was over, the group returned to the church and then their homes. The next day the following statement was read at a mass meeting:

> Don't worry about your children, they're gonna be all right. Don't hold them back if they want to go to jail. For they are doing a job not only for themselves, but for all of America and for all mankind. Somewhere we read, "A little child shall lead them." Remember there was another little child just twelve years old and he got involved in a discussion back in Jerusalem. He said, "I must be about my father's business." These young people are about their fathers' business. And they are carving a tunnel of hope through the great mountain of despair. We are going to see that they are treated right, don't worry about that...and go on and not only fill up the jails around here, but just fill up the jails all over the state of Alabama if necessary.[2]

> *"Like courage, fortitude is the ability to take emotion and turn it into energy for proactive, positive action."*

Prosperity Point

Fortitude is the quality of emotional core strength that feeds courageous actions. It doesn't mean we don't experience fear or other negative emotions, but that our faith and convictions take the upper hand, even when faced with harm. "Faith is a place of mystery, where we find the courage to believe in what we cannot see and the strength to let go of our fear of uncertainty," writes best-selling author, Dr. Brene Brown. So, like courage, fortitude is the ability to take emotion and turn it into energy for proactive, positive action. It's not mere talk, but a fire that burns within us to do what God has called us to do—to be a light in the darkness and a savory salt in a tasteless generation. As Brene Brown puts it, "Courage starts with showing up and letting ourselves be seen."

Prosperity Thought

Courage is the most important of all the virtues because without courage, you can't practice any other virtue consistently.
—Maya Angelou

Day Fourteen

HOPE

People tend to be generous when sharing their nonsense, fear, and ignorance. And while they seem quite eager to feed you their negativity, please remember that sometimes the diet we need to be on is a spiritual and emotional one. Be cautious with what you feed your mind and soul. Fuel yourself with positivity and let that fuel propel you into positive action.
—Steve Maraboli

While joy is the powerhouse that propels us forward, peace is the attitude with which we face every situation, and fortitude is the courage to do what is right regardless of the circumstances, none of these would do us any good without hope. What is hope? Hope is not only the optimism we need to stay positive in any given set of circumstances, hope is what frames our goals, anchors our faith, and gives us the confidence we need to take the next step even when everything seems against us.

In President Barack Obama's 2008 DNC Convention speech,[1] he urged constituents to "Hope in the face of difficulty. Hope in the face of uncertainty. The audacity of hope! In the end, that is God's greatest gift to us...a belief in things not seen. A belief that there are better days ahead." He also stated:

> Hope is what led a band of colonists to rise up against an empire; what led the greatest of generations to free a continent and heal a nation; what led young women

> and young men to sit at lunch counters and brave fire hoses and march through Selma and Montgomery for freedom's cause.
>
> Hope—hope is what led me here today—with a father from Kenya, a mother from Kansas, and a story that could only happen in the United States of America.
>
> Hope is the bedrock of this nation; the belief that our destiny will not be written for us, but by us; by all those men and women who are not content to settle for the world as it is; who have courage to remake the world as it should be.[2]

In one sense, hope is our blueprint. It allows us to idealize the future we want and set ourselves to pursue it as an earnestly expected goal. When we spend time meditating on what we *hope* to obtain, accomplish, or create, we generate a detailed image of what to invest our faith in. Faith then makes what we hope for real. Hebrews 11:1 goes so far as to tell us *"faith is the substance of things hoped for."* Hope gives us a vision of where we are headed, a design for the life we are crafting, and an outline of the calling and destiny we know God has for our lives.

"Hope gives us a vision of where we are headed, a design for the life we are crafting, and an outline of the calling and destiny we know God has for our lives."

At the same time, hope is a joyful and confident expectancy. Hope buoys optimism, but not just that things are going to work out, but that they are headed in a specific direction toward an anticipated end. It comes from steadfastly following God and repeatedly seeing His faithfulness. It should be founded in the repeated experience of God's goodness to us and our loved ones. As Paul expressed it: *"Endurance develops strength of character, and character strengthens our confident hope of salvation. And this hope will not lead to disappointment."*[3] Hope is not a silly sunniness that is in denial of the facts around us, rather it is an outlook based on a positive track record—we have been in bad situations before, and God has gotten us through. Why should what is happening to us now be any different?

Hope is also tied firmly to our knowing who we are in Christ and that our life has purpose. In Ephesians, Paul prayed *"that the eyes of your heart may be enlightened, so that you will know what is the hope of His calling."*[4] We hope ultimately in the promise of Heaven—going to live eternally in God's presence, escaping the confines of a world suffering from the lack of His presence. But we also hope as a person living on the earth with a mission from Him—living a life filled with commitment and fulfillment, seeing His presence burst into the lives of others and bringing light to their eyes—*"bringing in of a better hope, through which we draw near to God."*[5] Peter advised us that we should understand our purpose and calling—our hope—well enough to explain it to anyone who asks why we live so optimistically.

> *Do not fear their intimidation, and do not be troubled, but sanctify Christ as Lord in your hearts, always being ready to make a defense to everyone who asks you to give an account for the hope that is in you, yet with gentleness and reverence; and keep a good conscience so that in the thing in which you are slandered, those who revile your good behavior in Christ will be put to shame* (1 Peter 3:14-16 NASB).

Yet, the Bible speaks of hope—more often than any of these things—as something that we are to grab ahold of, to cling to, to speak out over our lives on a regular basis. The writer of Hebrews tells us, *"Christ as a Son over His own house, whose house we are if we hold fast the confidence and the rejoicing of the hope firm to the end,"*[6] and then again later that we should *"hold fast the confession of our hope without wavering, for He who promised is faithful."*[7] He tells us that our hope of Heaven, our hope of putting on Christ, and our hope of realizing His goodness, wisdom, and grace in our own lives should be an anchor to our souls, keeping us steadfast and safe, even in the stormiest of situations.

> *Thus God, determining to show more abundantly to the heirs of promise the immutability of His counsel, confirmed it by an oath, that by two immutable things, in which it is impossible for God to lie, we might have strong consolation, who have fled for refuge to lay hold of the hope set before us. This hope we have as an anchor of the soul, both sure and steadfast* (Hebrews 6:17-19).

This is one of the reasons I have written so many books that have declarations or prayers for readers to repeat daily. What we proclaim has power to change our lives, both affecting us as we confirm the hope we have for the future and charging our atmospheres with faith and confidence in God's promises. We must never underestimate the power of peppering our daily conversation with hope instead of despair and with faith instead of doubt. As Peter advised, *"Therefore, prepare your minds for action, keep sober in spirit, fix your hope completely on the grace to be brought to you at the revelation of Jesus Christ."*[8]

> ***"Hope is a perspective, an attitude, a battle plan, and a life preserver."***

In these ways, hope grounds us in the good things of God, keeping our eyes looking upward to see what God has for us on the horizon—instead of being downcast, focused only on the problems of today, or focused backward on the failures of yesterday. As the saying goes, you can't drive a car by only looking in the rearview mirror—or only at the speedometer, for that matter. We have to have our gaze looking up, focused forward, and hopeful about what the future is going to bring us.

Prosperity Point

We all need hope because hope is what keeps us alive. Faith depends on it—and with faith, we can move mountains. Hope is a perspective, an attitude, a battle plan, and a life preserver. We put it on, we meditate on it, and we are instructed repeatedly to grab ahold of it with both hands and hang on for dear life. To do these things is to keep our gaze upward where we can see the answers coming our way to whatever problems we face rather than downcast, focused on the problems alone. It is to ponder and proclaim with the psalmist:

> *Why am I discouraged? Why is my heart so sad? I will put my hope in God! I will praise him again—my Savior and my God!* (Psalm 42:11 NLT)

It is hope that enables us to look up in this way and *obtain* what we are looking for.

Prosperity Thought

Be kindly affectionate to one another with brotherly love, in honor giving preference to one another; not lagging in diligence, fervent in spirit, serving the Lord; rejoicing in hope, patient in tribulation, continuing steadfastly in prayer; distributing to the needs of the saints, given to hospitality (Romans 12:10-13).

Day Fifteen

TENACITY

Often it is tenacity, not talent, that rules the day.
—JULIA CAMERON,
Finding Water: The Art of Perseverance

The *Huffington Post* introduced the world to one of the most tenacious individuals I have read about in a while. His name is Stuart Scott. Long before this famous interview, sports fans knew him as an anchor for ESPN. Inside his martial arts studio, Stuart Scott lifted his black T-shirt that read, "Everyday I Fight." Beneath was a foot-long scar that bisected his washboard abs. "It's a sign of life," he said. It's the spot where cancer surgeons had opened his abdomen three times to remove cancerous tissue. He's had fifty-eight infusions of chemotherapy. He recently switched to a pill. But the drugs have not fully arrested the cancer that first struck in 2007 when his appendix was removed. It returned four years later and then again in 2013. Although each recurrence seemed more dire, after defeating each one, Scott returned to his high-profile work at ESPN. He has been viewed as a hero and an inspiration to many. He is far from faint-hearted.

In a very similar way, the pursuit of God is not for the faint of heart or the fickle. Neither is the pursuit of what God puts into your heart. You must fight opposing forces within and without—and sometimes the forces within are greater than those without!

Harvard Professor Angela Ducksworth has concluded that the key to a successful and prosperous life is not a matter of talent, but "grit." She states, "There are many talented individuals who simply do not follow through on their commitments. In fact, in our data, grit is usually unrelated or even inversely related to measures of talent." So what exactly is "grit," you may ask? "Grit is sticking with your future—day in, day out, not just for the week, not just for the month, but for years—and working really hard to make that future a reality."[1]

What kind of soul do you imagine is able to exercise that type of grit? Did Joseph exemplify grit? What do you think exemplifies a great hero? Is grit required for success, or victory, or before that big payoff comes?

Great battles that require great measures of grit are what make for great heroes. To win a battle takes tenacity. As the warrior Winston Churchill once said, "Never give in—never, never, never, never, in nothing great or small, large or petty, never give in except to convictions of honor and good sense. Never yield to force; never yield to the apparently overwhelming might of the enemy."

> *Great battles that require great measures of grit are what make for great heroes.*

There is virtue in being steadfast and consistent. It is this type of virtue that enabled the tortoise to beat the hare in a foot race. It is the attitude of the itsy, bitsy spider who refuses to stop climbing no matter how many times it gets knocked down the spout. It is the dogged determination of the scientist in the quest for discovery, of the inventor for innovation, and the lover for the beloved. It is a key characteristic of anyone who finds what they are looking for.[2]

God Himself expressed that it was the key to finding the future and hope that we wish to obtain from Him. He encouraged those thirsty for Him with these words through the prophet Jeremiah:

> *For I know the thoughts that I think toward you, says the Lord, thoughts of peace and not of evil, to give you a future and a hope. Then you will call upon Me and go and pray to*

> *Me, and I will listen to you. And you will seek Me and find Me, when you search for Me with all your heart* (Jeremiah 29:11-13).

Jesus echoed this in the Gospel of Matthew:

> *Ask, and it will be given to you; seek, and you will find; knock, and it will be opened to you. For everyone who asks receives, and he who seeks finds, and to him who knocks it will be opened. Or what man is there among you who, if his son asks for bread, will give him a stone? Or if he asks for a fish, will he give him a serpent? If you then, being evil, know how to give good gifts to your children, how much more will your Father who is in heaven give good things to those who ask Him!* (Matthew 7:7-11)

We are all pretty good at asking, but what if the receiving doesn't come easily? What if we ask, and then ask again, and then feel we need to ask again, and don't seem to be getting what we are after? What if we seem to come to a stop sign smack dab in the middle of the road we feel God has called us to follow? What are we to do then?

This is the exact problem that characterized those who became known as the "Christian mystics." These Renaissance Christians wanted to focus their lives on connecting with God in very real ways. They were called *mystics* because they wanted to delve into and understand the *mysteries* of God. Many of them chose to close themselves off in monasteries and nunneries to devote their lives to prayer and experiencing the presence of God.

In comparing their writings, one will find that all of them seemed to experience a common pattern that they expressed as a series of wildernesses or plateaus. They would come into wonderfully full times of experiencing the presence of God where they heard His voice quite clearly, and then they would experience a period when it seemed God had almost completely abandoned them. They would hit "dry spells" in their prayer pursuits, as if they had just wandered from a lush forest where there was abundant fruit onto a barren, dry expanse that looked as if it went on without end. These desert or wilderness times would test their resolve and their faith. Would they go on? Had God abandoned them? Had they done something wrong that they needed to repent of? Why was God suddenly silent?

So they dug deeper. They persevered. They tenaciously continued their pursuit of God, asking Him what they needed to do to adjust their path. They studied their Bibles, they experimented with new ways of praise and worship, and they fasted. In this process, they eventually came to new breakthroughs—new heights of experiencing God's goodness—an even more lush place in the presence of God than they'd experienced before. The process wasn't an easy one, but once they got through to the other side of the plateau and they found themselves again rising to another level, they were oh-so-glad they had continued the pursuit.

It may seem strange, since God can literally do anything He wants, but it often doesn't seem as important for Him to make His presence known on the earth as it does for Him to make it known through His children. It may seem like a divine hide and seek on the surface, but what it actually does, as we press in to seek Him, is shape us and build into us the characteristics we need to handle His mysteries correctly. This process, in many ways, is God's crucible for purifying our motives and honing our abilities—His pottery wheel for molding us into vessels fit for His most precious secrets, whether they be spiritual, scientific, entrepreneurial, artistic, educational, political, or in whatever arena He wants our lives to touch the world. As Paul described it to Timothy:

> *In a great house there are not only vessels of gold and silver, but also of wood and clay, some for honor and some for dishonor. Therefore if anyone cleanses himself from the latter,*

> *he will be a vessel for honor, sanctified and useful for the Master, prepared for every good work* (2 Timothy 2:20-21).

So what we do when we "get stuck" or come to these roadblocks makes all the difference. Do we give up believing God has something different for us, even though it was His prompting that led us to this point? Do we compromise, choosing to put on a godly outer appearance while neglecting our true calling as something beyond our abilities? Or do we press on, reevaluating our approach and doing whatever we can to proceed more creatively and wisely? Do we accept the stumbling block as an obstacle impossible to overcome, a place to settle down and spend the rest of our lives, or a place to reevaluate, press ourselves to be more than we were in the past, and then find God's way beyond the obstacle to greater things ahead?

Prosperity Point

Very few of the most successful people in our world are the most talented, intelligent, or gifted. Every big fish gets into a pool of other fish who are just as talented, just as smart, and just as artistic—and many see that not as a challenge to press through and make themselves better, but as an indication that they don't have what it takes to succeed in that arena. The tenacious, however, even if they are not the most talented, intelligent, or gifted, stay the course and develop the skills they need to succeed. Thus, it is not necessarily the qualities that we are born with that will take us where we feel destined to go, but the character traits and resilience we pick up along the way. As Solomon warned us:

> *The race is not to the swift, nor the battle to the strong, nor bread to the wise, nor riches to men of understanding, nor favor to men of skill; but time and chance happen to them all* (Ecclesiastes 9:11).

What we do with that time and chance makes all the difference.

Prosperity Thought

Many of life's failures are people who did not realize how close they were to success when they gave up.
—Thomas A. Edison

Week Four

PHYSICAL PROSPERITY

The greatest wealth is health.
—VIRGIL

Day Sixteen

THE SOUL-BODY CONNECTION

A merry heart does good, like medicine,
but a broken spirit dries the bones
(Proverbs 17:22).

There is a seldom recognized error we fall into when we discuss that human beings are made in the image of God in three parts: spirit, soul, and body. What we tend to do in talking about these three aspects of who we are is spend a great deal of time trying to differentiate one from the other so that we can understand what parts of us are spirit, what functions are in the soul, and how those affect the physical bodies through which we encounter the physical universe. We liken it to the three very distinct persons of the Godhead: the Father, the Son, and the Holy Spirit. But then we also know that God is not three but one—however, that is such a hard concept to visualize that we put that truth on the back burner and get on with what seem more pertinent matters.

Well, the fact is that while we are a tripartite being—comprised of a spirit, soul, and body—a spirit that has contact with the spiritual realm and God, a body that has contact with the physical realm and other people, and our souls that make up our personalities, mind, will, and emotions—we are also one. For example, every thought we have in our minds (soul) has a physical expression in the prefrontal cortex of our brains (body). Every emotion (soul) we feel is also expressed as very real, physical, chemical interactions in our limbic and nervous systems (body). Every decision of the will (soul) not only results in physical action, but will also affect our moods, perspective, and attitudes, setting off physical triggers in our bodies. The more science looks into it, the more direct connections they are finding between the mind, will, and emotions, and sickness, disease, energy levels, attention spans, balance, appetite, and other things one would think were purely physical.

For example, research has found that chronic loneliness—which is on the rise according to a recent Barna poll (today one in five people report experiencing loneliness as opposed to just one in six a few years ago)—can be as toxic to the length of your life as smoking. With statistics showing that roughly 20 percent of the population feels severely lonely at any one time, medical scientists are starting to consider this a significant risk factor. Long-term feelings of loneliness appear to increase the number of stress hormones and affect the way we respond to social stimuli. That begins a chain reaction resulting in a downward negative spiral of social, emotional, and physical disease. The added chronic stress increases inflammation in the body—a major risk factor in heart disease—and decreases immune system response. It appears to put our bodies into a state of increased susceptibility to illness that, over time, will knock years off of the length of our lives. As novelist John Steinbeck once expressed it, "A sad soul can kill you quicker, far quicker, than a germ."

Now that's just the power of one toxic emotion, and a relatively nonviolent one. Imagine what the impact is on our health to live in constant negativity where verbal abuse is handed out frequently. Imagine the effects of ongoing frustration, anger, unforgiveness, cruelty, distrust, unfaithfulness, hopelessness, unrest, hostility, etc. No wonder we in America—even though we set the standard for being a "developed" nation—still have some of the most chronic health problems in the world. Certainly there are other factors as well—we do tend to eat the wrong kinds of foods, live lives that are too sedentary, expose ourselves to too much violence in our entertainment, carry too much stress about things that are relatively insignificant, and the like—but it isn't hard to see that even resolving these starts with changing our mind; reorienting parts of our soul.

The good news is that while scientific research is finding that there can be great harm done to our bodies by an unhealthy soul, there can also be great good done if we prosper our souls. In fact, while the research of the twentieth century concluded that our personalities and temperaments were greatly determined by our first five years of life, more scientific and advanced research of the brain in the last decade has determined we can do much more to change our habits and tendencies than we ever thought possible. The science of neuroplasticity ("neuro" like neuron, having to do with our "thinking" cells; and "plasticity" having to do with the malleable or "plastic" nature of our brain) is finding we can, in fact, quite literally "change our minds" by thinking new thoughts—and rewire our brains by forming new mental habits that default to more positive perspectives. Think for a moment of the health benefits that are locked up in the fruit of the Spirit: *"Love, joy, peace, longsuffering, kindness, goodness, faithfulness, gentleness, self-control."*[1]

> *"Deep within our minds God has locked up unfathomable possibilities."*

Deep within our minds—and reflected in our physical brains—God has locked up virtually unfathomable possibilities[2]—and researchers are finding that we have far more control over the process of choosing those possibilities than we previously understood. Let's consider again the following description of the brain given in a TED Talk by Dr. Vilayanur S. Ramachandran, Director of the Center for the Brain and Cognition at the University of California, San Diego:

> Here is this three-pound mass of jelly you can hold in the palm of your hand. It can contemplate the vastness

> of interstellar space. It can contemplate the meaning of infinity—ask questions about the meaning of its own existence and about the nature of God.... It is the greatest mystery confronting human beings. How does this all come about?
>
> As you know, the brain is made up of neurons. There are 100 billion neurons in the adult human brain and each neuron makes something like 1,000 to 10,000 contacts with other neurons in the brain. Based on this people have calculated that the number of permutations and combinations of brain activity exceeds *the number of elementary particles in the universe* [my emphasis].

Now, that's not the number of molecules in the universe, but the number of elementary particles that join together *to make* molecules!

Are you limited in who you can become? Not even close! New choices lead to new neural pathways, new habits, a different, more prosperous you, as well as new discoveries, innovations, breakthroughs, and so many more good things! You have the power of change built right into your very soul—shouldn't you be more mindful of taking advantage of it?

Prosperity Point

While we can certainly implement different habits that will contribute to our bodies being more prosperous and healthy—how we eat, how we exercise, how much we rest, etc.—the truth of the matter is that none of that will do as much good as finding better patterns of being on the level of our souls. If there are things that you are struggling with physically, ask God what might be buried in your soul that is contributing to those problems and what new attitudes, outlooks, thoughts, and truths you need to plant firmly in your heart to remedy your dis-ease.

Prosperity Thought

> *Don't copy the behavior and customs of this world, but let God transform you into a new person by changing the way you think. Then you will learn to know God's will for you, which is good and pleasing and perfect* (Romans 12:2 NLT).

Day Seventeen

SELF-CONTROL

Those who are at the mercy of impulse—who lack self-control—suffer moral deficiency: The ability to control impulse is the base of will and character.
—DANIEL GOLEMAN,
Emotional Intelligence

As we saw in the last chapter, not only will lack of self-control lead to "moral deficiency" as Daniel Goleman points out in the opening quote, but it will also lead to physical problems as well. Wrong attitudes leave psychological and physiological footprints in the chemical interactions and systems of our bodies—sometimes blocking proper operations and other times increasing the production of "emergency reaction measures" that have long-term negative effects. So, if I were going to pick one factor that would help us prosper our bodies in the long run for the sake of living a full, energized, joyful, long life, it would be exercising the spiritual muscle of self-control.

Daniel Goleman gave us a new picture of the power of self-control in his best seller, *Emotional Intelligence.* In the book, he defines emotional intelligence as "self-control, zeal, and persistence, and the ability to motivate oneself."[1] One of the most powerful indicators of emotional intelligence is the ability to delay gratification—to "trade" a short-term reward for a greater one down the road.

To demonstrate the effects of this, researchers posed what has become known as the "marshmallow challenge" to a group of four-year-olds from the Stanford University day care. They told each child that the investigator needed to run an errand and would be back in a little while. If the child waited patiently, he or she could have two marshmallows when the researcher returned, or the child could have one marshmallow right now. The researcher would then leave the "down payment" marshmallow with them and leave the room not to return for fifteen to twenty minutes. Some, as you would guess, grabbed and gobbled down their single marshmallow within seconds of the researcher leaving. Those with more self-restraint waited out the time, often coming up with clever strategies to make the time pass more quickly. Some covered their eyes to keep from being tempted by seeing the marshmallow, some put down their heads or tried to sleep. Others sang, played games with their hands and feet, or talked to themselves to help the time pass more quickly. Those who resisted the one marshmallow were promptly rewarded with two when the researcher returned.

> *"One of the most powerful indicators of emotional intelligence is the ability to delay gratification."*

Now, this may seem like a simple little test, but there were surprising results when the researchers tracked down the same children fourteen years later as they were preparing for high school gradation. The difference between the one-marshmallow-now teens and the we-can-wait-to-get-two-marshmallows-later group was dramatic. The group that could wait proved to be marked by greater social competence: They were more personally effective, self-assertive, and better able to cope with the frustrations of life. They embraced challenges and pursued solutions energetically; they took initiative and plunged into projects. Not only that, but they also scored significantly higher on their SAT tests, on average scoring roughly 210 points higher in their overall scores. When compared with their IQs at age four, delayed gratification proved to be twice as effective of a predictor for what their SAT scores would be.[2]

Dr. Goleman wrote the following about the study:

> What Walter Mischel, who did the study, describes with the rather infelicitous phrase "goal-directed self-imposed delay of gratification" is perhaps the essence of emotional self-regulation: The ability to deny impulse in the service of a goal, whether it be building a business, solving an algebraic equation, or pursuing the Stanley Cup. His finding underscores the role of emotional intelligence as a meta-ability, determining how well or how poorly people are able to use their own mental capacities.[3]

Once again, we see that it is not necessarily how smart or how talented we are that determines our success, nor is it simply chance. We can, instead, dramatically up the odds for success by practicing traits that can be learned, such as self-control. In the long run, these are better indicators that we will do well—and enjoy life while doing it—than the natural giftings or attributes we are born with. That is not to say that natural giftings and inborn attributes aren't wonderful things and indicators of the destiny God has for us, but the smart guy who spends all of his time playing video games will always eventually fall behind the kid with the lower IQ who chooses to struggle through his homework first before playing. Self-restraint will not only keep him from harm, but also propel him toward success. King Solomon said it this way in Proverbs 25:28, *"A person without self-control is like a city with broken-down walls"* (NLT). Without self-control, we are susceptible to whatever scam or harm temptation wants to bring our way. Self-control creates healthy constraints that keeps wrong influences out and keeps us better focused on doing what needs to be done.

> *"Long-term vision is the platform upon which we build short-term action."*

The marshmallow test also gives us a key to developing self-control. We need to break down our actions into immediate and long-range rewards, and practice choosing the latter. This means we put work before pleasure, exercise before relaxing, reading before television, prayer before gossip, virtue before vice, and the like, every time. But it also means we use self-control to practice wholeness. We don't overwork, sacrificing family time and health to inch ahead in our careers hoping for greater prestige and higher salaries. No, we use self-control to manage our health for strength, energy, and long life; our money to be enough to care for all of our real needs; our time and skills to increase the value of each minute we work; and how we rest and recreate in order to get the most out of our family times to truly recharge our batteries.

Prosperity Point

The key to self-control is the ability to visualize the benefit of long-term achievement over short-term gratification. The more time we spend meditating on the things of God, on the goals we have set for ourselves in each realm of life, on the calling we have from God and the objectives we should be pursing each day to work toward it, the easier self-control will be to exercise because we will see the value of the trade-offs. I like how the New American Standard Bible expresses it in Proverbs 29:18, *"Where there is no vision, the people are unrestrained."* Long-term vision is the platform upon which we build short-term action. We must exercise self-control to pick tomorrow's triumphs over today's struggles, pains, and instant gratifications. It is the basis for physical prosperity, as well as prosperity in every other realm.

Prosperity Thought

Better to be patient than powerful; better to have self-control than to conquer a city (Proverbs 16:32 NLT).

Day Eighteen

EXERCISE AND NUTRITION

Good for the body is the work of the body, and
good for the soul is the work of the soul, and
good for either is the work of the other.
—Henry David Thoreau

When God created humankind, I don't think He had a sedentary lifestyle for us in mind. Eden was a place without couches or chairs, and where there was plenty of food available—all of it organic! We were created to be active—to walk, run, and generally be doing something outside all, if not most, of the time. He planned that we would eat *real* food, not nutrient-depleted from a box. God even said, *"You may freely eat"*[1] of everything He provided for food. There were no dietary restrictions! (Only a moral one: Not to eat of the tree of the knowledge of good and evil.)

We were designed to be healthiest and happiest when we are fit, eat good food, and get the sleep we need. Doing this gives us energy, increases our ability to focus and be productive, as well as makes us feel better about the person we are. This allows us to project ourselves more positively onto the world around us, to be more resilient against disease and criticism, and enables us to stay the course more resolutely when the going gets tough.

Oh, if it were only that easy.

Today's world is far from that idyllic state of an abundant paradise. We have unhealthy food temptations that never existed in the Garden, and the demands of a modern lifestyle—that for most of us—involves sitting inside and staring at a screen all day. At the same time, what we eat, even if it's "whole food," has become a challenge due to how it's farmed and distributed. Furthermore, because we don't take time to prepare and appreciate our food as we were meant to, we tend to put it off and then eat whatever is most convenient. That is especially tough on someone like me who is constantly traveling and eating in restaurants. I think God meant us to have a closer relationship with our food than modern society encourages. We are supposed to enjoy our food from the selection, through the preparation, to the eating of it together with others. As Ecclesiastes 3:13 tells us, *"Every man* [and woman] *should eat and drink and enjoy the good of all his labor—it is the gift of God."* If this weren't a basic human instinct, all those cooking shows wouldn't be the most watched of any shows on television!

One of the problems we face is that instead of learning about food, its benefits, how to enjoy preparing it, which foods prosper our health and which impoverish it, and the like, we get into a war with food that twists our relationship with it. Instead of learning to maximize the enjoyment of each bite and savoring what is enough, we tend to work until we are famished then overindulge. We don't command our appetites; we are instead their slaves.

When food is in charge of us rather than the other way around, we pay a high price. As Irish scholar and educator Thomas Moffett put it, "We are digging our grave with our teeth." The story of Esau in the Bible may be an extreme example of this, but because he didn't plan his meals, allowing him to eat on a regular schedule, it cost him dearly!

> *Now Jacob cooked a stew; and Esau came in from the field, and he was weary. And Esau said to Jacob, "Please feed me with that same red stew, for I am weary." Therefore his name was called Edom. But Jacob said, "Sell me your birthright*

as of this day." And Esau said, "Look, I am about to die; so what is this birthright to me?" Then Jacob said, "Swear to me as of this day." So he swore to him, and sold his birthright to Jacob. And Jacob gave Esau bread and stew of lentils; then he ate and drank, arose, and went his way. Thus Esau despised his birthright (Genesis 25:29-34).

Esau found himself in a place where he was vulnerable to temptation with regard to food because he was tired, hungry, and had made no plans for what he was going to eat when he got home from "work" that day. Not only that, but he made the mistake of walking by something that smelled good—in his case it was his brother's homemade stew that he loved so much he was nicknamed after it! For us it might be a fast-food restaurant, a deli, even a donut shop. Esau was weak and vulnerable. He started thinking something like, "You know, there's no need to make my own dinner—here it is already prepared! I'm so hungry! Why don't I just stop here and eat some of this before I fall down dead of starvation!"

> *"Any problem of restraint is essentially a problem of vision."*

By this time, it didn't matter that the price his brother asked of him was exorbitant. He was hungry, and his appetite controlled him rather than the other way around. He wanted to eat his favorite food, no matter the cost! So, he gave up his birthright. Just how dumb can you get? No self-control whatsoever!

The Bible tells us that in this way, Esau *despised* his birthright. He didn't recognize its worth. He rejected the plan of God for his life. He had no esteem for his future, no plan to prosper his estate, no vision for extending and prospering the blessings of God on his family. As a result, he was willing to trade his birthright away for a bowl of soup. How very true it is that *"where there is no vision, the people perish."*[2]

Any problem of restraint—any problem that is caused by us doing, or not doing, certain things—is essentially a problem of vision. If we find ourselves continually failing at changing our behavior toward something we want to accomplish, it is because the vision we hold for what we want to obtain is not strong enough. As I have heard many success coaches say, "Change rarely happens until the pain of staying the same is greater than the pain of changing." Vision is a big part of helping that change process. Until we begin to see ourselves as the person we want to become rather than the person trapped where we are now, we will never create the emotional energy toward change that will help us transform ourselves or eliminate the behaviors that are keeping us from who we want to become.

We need to visualize the person we want to be, create a step-by-step plan toward being that person, and then find ways to monitor our progress and encourage ourselves as we make the incremental steps toward fulfilling that vision. Esau was not a man of vision, nor was he a man of good planning, and it cost him. What is it costing you not to have a plan about your physical health?

Prosperity Point

Food and fitness are a lot like money in that either they serve us to accomplish what we want, or we serve them. Are you getting the fulfillment God intended for you to have from what you eat and what you do? Or is your relationship with food and exercise causing unwanted complications? If so, get a vision for who God has created you to be, create a plan for how to be that person, and get after it day by day, meal by meal, and training session by training session. You will be so glad you did!

Prosperity Thought

Everyone runs; one wins. Run to win. All good athletes train hard. They do it for a gold medal that tarnishes and fades. You're after one that's gold eternally. I don't know about you, but I'm running hard for the finish line. I'm giving it everything I've got. No sloppy living for me! I'm staying alert and in top condition (1 Corinthians 9:24-27 MSG).

Day Nineteen

REST

Jesus said, "Come to me, all of you who are weary and carry heavy burdens, and I will give you rest. Take my yoke upon you. Let me teach you, because I am humble and gentle at heart, and you will find rest for your souls. For my yoke is easy to bear, and the burden I give you is light" (Matthew 11:28-30 NLT).

How are you at the end of the day? Frazzled? Fatigued? Dragging yourself home to eat, spending a little time with your family before zoning out in front of the TV, then falling into bed to get up the next morning and start the cycle all over again?

If that's you, I've got good news for you: God has something better in mind!

You see, the rhythm of life God wanted for us as human beings—working, resting, eating, sleeping, parenting, socializing, etc.—He expressed in the very first verses of the Bible, the very first actions He chose to share with humanity. The seven-day cycle we call a "week" is a reminder of God's rhythm for life. Every week that we live should hold at least a little of the wonder of the world's first week. It was a pattern He meant us to celebrate, enjoy, and repeat.

First of all, the work that God did that first week was both creative—yes, quite literally!—and exhilarating. He had a picture in mind that He was working toward, and there was purpose in everything that He did. The prophet Isaiah asked:

> *Who has measured the waters in the hollow of His hand, measured heaven with a span and calculated the dust of the earth in a measure? Weighed the mountains in scales and the hills in a balance?* (Isaiah 40:12)

Before He spoke the first words of creation, God took a drop of water in His hand and determined the qualities and properties He would put into it so that it would sustain life. He designated it as a transportation system for everything from soil to organisms. He calculated its ideal density, polarity, viscosity, and composition. He determined how it would change state to create the water cycle and at what temperature it would freeze. He designed it in such a way so that when it froze, the ice would cling to the top of a body of water preserving the life beneath, rather than sink to the bottom and freeze everything in it. He determined every attribute before He released the first molecule of it into the universe. Why? Because it served a purpose.

> *"The idea of rest is a more perplexing one than most of us have ever stopped to consider."*

Though we probably never think of it, planning was a big part of the rhythm of creation. And proper planning meant that not only did God know what He was going to create and do in those first six days, but He also knew He would be finished on the sixth day so He could rest on the seventh. As Genesis 2:2 tells us, *"On the seventh day God ended His work which He had done, and He rested."* Rest has a purpose. It is in our rest state that the body rejuvenates itself.

Not only did God rest on the seventh day, creating the Sabbath—what we today call the "weekend"—but at the end of each day He knew when it would be time to set down His work, look back over the day, and see that it was good. Neither the work of the day before nor His plans for what He would create the next day interfered with being able to stop in the evening, look over what He had done, and pronounce that *"it was good."*[1]

In a world where there is always too much to do, the idea of rest—and I don't just mean sleep, but taking time to be quiet, calm, *and rest*—is a more perplexing one than most of us have ever stopped to consider.

I recently read an article highlighting the work of sleep by specialist Dr. Matthew Edlund. In it he suggested, "If you can't sleep, a rest can be just as curative as sleep. Many of us are so busy we see rest as a weakness—a waste of precious time—but rest is, in fact, a biological need. All the science shows we need rest to live, just like we need food." Dr. Edlund described four different kinds of active rest: social, mental, physical, and spiritual.

He defined social rest as spending time with friends and relations or even chatting with colleagues. Making small talk with friends was shown to reduce stress hormone levels and provide psychological benefits. Indeed, most researchers agree that social connections are as significant to your longevity and the quality of your life as obesity and smoking are harmful.

Mental rest is the calming of the mind. It has been shown to affect the nervous system as well as change blood pressure, heart rate, and body temperature. The key to mental rest is to get so engrossed in something simple that you effectively escape your troubles or daily concerns.

Physical rest includes getting adequate sleep and napping for fifteen to thirty minutes during the day. According to a NASA study, napping cuts your risk of heart attack by 37 percent and improves work performance on some tasks by as much as 38 percent.[2]

Spiritual rest is also a necessity for overall health. Brain scans have shown that people who meditate are able to physically expand parts of their brains and even increase the size of their frontal lobes, the part that controls concentration, attention, and focus—and where we do much of our problem solving. Those who meditate also build up more grey matter in the midbrain, where functions such as breathing and blood circulation are managed, as well as improve the dorsolateral prefrontal cortex, which is important to memory and muscle coordination. Prolonged meditation also affects the structure of the thalamus, a part of the brain critical for processing information flow from all parts of the body.

Praying, though more active than meditation, is also recognized as spiritual rest. Brain scans have shown that prayer provides benefits similar to meditation. Research has also shown that people who regularly attend religious services live longer than those who do not, although some of the benefit may be due to the social connection rather than the services themselves.[3]

In learning God's rhythm of grace, we must also learn His rhythm of rest. It starts with trusting Him more than our own efforts—and in being like Moses: Anytime he faced a difficult situation or controversy, the first thing he did was pull away to pray in order to hear what God had to say. He knew to take whatever concern he had at the moment and leave it with God. He knew how to take the cares and responsibilities of the great leadership he was entrusted with into prayer and to not leave that place of prayer until he had attained God's peace and His rest.

The rhythms of our days should be the same. We should have a plan for where we are going in life in each of its eight realms, for what we are going to do in each of those areas every day, and be able to come to the end of each day, and say, "That was good." Then we should be able to set our heads down on our pillows at night ready to enjoy getting enough sleep, because we are looking forward to getting up the next morning and seeing what new adventures God has in store.

Prosperity Point

We do not get the rest we need if we are not living in God's cycles of grace, trust, obedience, and creative enjoyment in the tasks of each day.

We live in a stressful world—a world in which people are running to and fro, pushing harder, and working longer hours. Most people have two jobs and then have to go home and cook and clean and take care of this and that. We have now become a neurotic people—pulling out our hair—frustrated and confused. Many people have stopped relaxing, recreating, exercising, and even eating properly. Fast food, microwaves, and other convenience-oriented appliances hold the promise of saving us time—yet we have less and less time for family, worship, meditation, prayer, and things that refresh and recharge us.

If you are overtaxed, if you feel like you are burning out, it is time to look at how you are doing in each of the eight realms of life and repurpose your weekly routine. Each day should have its time to rest, just as each week should. Make sure you take time aside physically, emotionally, and mentally to obey God's edict to *"cease striving and know that I am God."*[4]

PROSPERITY THOUGHT

God's promise of entering his rest still stands, so we ought to tremble with fear that some of you might fail to experience it. For this good news—that God has prepared this rest—has been announced to us just as it was to them. But it did them no good because they didn't share the faith of those who listened to God (Hebrews 4:1-2 NLT).

Day Twenty

PURITY

Beloved, now we are children of God, and it has not appeared as yet what we will be. We know that when He appears, we will be like Him, because we will see Him just as He is. And everyone who has this hope fixed on Him purifies himself, just as He is pure
(1 John 3:2-3 NASB).

What good is sinlessness if forgiveness is available? What good is purity—sticking to the letter of God's law, if you will—if "it is easier to ask forgiveness than to ask permission"? Isn't that just being legalistic and judgmental? What does it really matter anyway? What is the value of living "purely"? What difference does it make?

An online article from *Christianity Today* discussed how much press Olympic hurdler Lolo Jones and Heisman Trophy winner Tim Tebow were receiving about their declarations that they were virgins.[1] The article discussed how strange it is in our culture today for someone to choose to remain celibate deep into their twenties and even early thirties. Recent movies like *The 40-Year-Old Virgin* seem to be a case in point, implying that if you are still a virgin by that point, you must have some serious, psychosocial deficiencies. The article also discussed how challenging it is to remain celibate until we are married and how little support for it there seems to be to do so in the Church today—mainly, perhaps, because the Church seems to speak so little about sexuality as a whole. It was an interesting, if inconclusive, discussion.

But then I was surprised further to read that many of the comments about the article blatantly challenged the idea that celibacy really mattered at all. After all, was there going to be some kind of medal ceremony in Heaven for all those who remained virgins until they were married or chose a life of singleness as priests and nuns do? Was there some special reward for those who remained pure distinguishing them from those who indulged themselves and then asked for forgiveness later? If God really does toss our mistakes and disobedience into the sea of forgetfulness and remove our transgressions from us *"as far as the east is from the west,"*[2] why does purity matter?

"It's not always reasonable to choose to follow God; it is a matter of desperate, unreasonable love."

Those are reasonable questions. But then, as George Bernard Shaw wrote, "The reasonable man adapts himself to the world; the unreasonable one persists in trying to adapt the world to himself. Therefore all progress depends on the unreasonable man." After all, it's not always reasonable to choose to follow God; it is a matter of desperate, unreasonable love.

Now, first of all, though I have used sexual purity as the example here, I am not just talking about purity as it relates to our sexuality. To be pure is to choose God's way over the world's way in everything we do. It is to keep the tabernacle of God undefiled.[3] Purity is an issue of the heart.[4] It is to choose selflessness in following God over selfishness *every time.* It has to do with the food we eat, the thoughts we think, the entertainment we allow into our homes and minds, the way we speak, how we conduct ourselves when relating to others, how we take care of our bodies, and so much more. Sexuality, in this regard, is just an example, though it is a poignant one.

Second, yes, we all make mistakes in following God, and none of us could make it without forgiveness. "There, but for the grace of God..." as the saying goes. None of us can throw the first stone, as none of us has made it through life without stumbling in some area.

But, at the same time, none of these are an excuse for compromise. Whatever you allow to compromise your values as you climb the ladder of success will attempt to control you once you're at the top.

If we have an assignment from God on this earth and a divine purpose to accomplish for the Kingdom of Heaven, then our path should be one of choosing purity in all things regardless of whether we understand why or not. If we are going to follow a path, it is only logical that sticking to that path without deviation is going to get us to our ultimate goal faster than if we only stuck to it part of the time.

In the passage from 1 John that I shared at the beginning of this chapter, John states, in essence, that we choose to purify ourselves because of the hope we have of one day being like Jesus. Once again, to choose purity over compromise is a matter of vision. The better our vision of where we are going, the better we'll stick to our plan to get there. Oswald Chambers described it this way:

"Every action of the common day that we take either leads us closer to our destiny or farther from it."

> If the spiritual bloom of our life with God is getting impaired in the tiniest degree, we must leave off everything and get it put right. Remember that vision depends on character—*the pure in heart* see God.[5]

To walk in purity is to walk in singleness of purpose, with our eyes open, pursuing God and what He wants for us above all else.

I'd like to be able to say that there will be some huge, obvious difference made in your life because you chose to walk purely before God. I would love to be able to say that it is some kind of mystical, divine shortcut to realizing the perfect will of God for your life. Wouldn't it be wonderful if I could say that purity is going to lead you to great clarity in hearing His voice, revelatory dreams and visions, or other wonderful supernatural manifestations in your life? But I can't. The path each of us follows in obedience to God isn't always marked with milestones like those. We won't be able to look back on this side of Heaven and say things like, "Oh, because I stayed obedient to God during that time, I got to my goals five years faster." Maybe someday God will show us what good it did for us to walk purely before Him, but, until then, all I know is that He holds the keys to where I want to be! Why would I want to deviate into disobedience knowing any pleasures of being selfish will not only be temporary, but will slow me down? As Christ said in the book of Revelation:

> *I advise you to buy from Me gold refined by fire so that you may become rich, and white garments so that you may clothe yourself, and that the shame of your nakedness will not be revealed; and eye salve to anoint your eyes so that you may see* (Revelation 3:18 NASB).

Prosperity Point

Our Christian walk is one of capacity and character building. Oscar Wilde wrote, "Every little action of the common day makes or unmakes character." In the same way, every action of the common day that we take either leads us closer to our destiny or farther from it. To choose impurity is to choose cloudy vision. It is to despise our purpose and the grace of God—like Esau despising his birthright. To live purely, sexually and otherwise, is not to deny ourselves something good, but to choose to live for something better. It is to choose love over selfishness and self-control over self-indulgence. It is not only to choose where we ultimately want to be over where we are at the moment, but also to exercise the emotional intelligence so key to our success in all areas of life. It is to accept God's timing and rhythms of grace for our lives, trusting fully that He knows what He is doing.

Prosperity Thought

Always aim at complete harmony of thought and word and deed. Always aim at purifying your thoughts and everything will be well.
—Mahatma Gandhi

Week Five

RELATIONAL PROSPERITY

The meeting of two personalities is like the contact of two chemical substances: if there is any reaction, both are transformed.
—C.G. JUNG

Day Twenty-One

EMPATHY

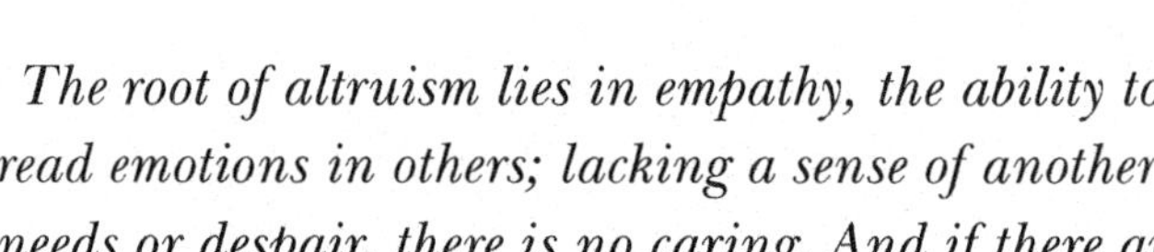

The root of altruism lies in empathy, the ability to read emotions in others; lacking a sense of another's needs or despair, there is no caring. And if there are two moral stances that our times call for, they are precisely these, self-restraint and compassion.

—DANIEL GOLEMAN,
Emotional Intelligence

True empathy has two parts: 1) the ability to "step into another's shoes," so to speak, seeing what life looks like from that person's perspective; and 2) a deep conviction that, despite all appearances, the person is competent enough to be responsible for his or her own life. The ability to step into the other person's shoes is sympathy; the ability to trust the person and not to do for him or her what the person can do for him- or herself is respect.

Sympathy without recognizing dignity has a tendency to create dependency and entitlement; respect without sympathy has a way of hardening our hearts and making us callous to the suffering of others, often causing us to become legalistic. Empathy, however, recognizes both need and competency. Where sympathy alone will do for others, empathy will step in beside them and do just enough until they can take care of themselves. Where confidence in the abilities of others alone will often overlook the severity of a need, empathy will get into the struggle with them and not leave until they are back on their feet. Empathy helps, empathy teaches, empathy loves, and empathy empowers. The goal of empathy is to come alongside those in crisis and walk with them until the two can stand side by side at journey's end.

Jesus was a great example of empathy. He was the ultimate empowerment specialist.

Throughout the Gospels we see that Jesus was moved by compassion for the afflicted and oppressed. Yet if we look at some of the individual interactions He had with the sick or disabled, He always showed the deepest respect for their jurisdiction over their own lives and bodies. He would often ask something like, *"What do you want Me to do for you?"*[1]—not willing to overstep the authority they held over their lives. He would do whatever He could to activate the person's faith, so once they left Him, they would have a new ability to connect with God on their own. We see Jesus step in to see that justice is done when the woman caught in adultery was brought to Him for sentencing in John 8, but after He has shown mercy, we also see Him ask for accountability by directing her to *"go and sin no more."*[2]

He often also asked for some step of faith on behalf of the other person, giving specific instructions that would unlock the power of God through obedience. When His disciples asked Him about a man born blind who they passed by, Jesus didn't just reach out and heal him as part of His final answer to their questions, but instead:

> *He spat on the ground and made clay with the saliva; and He anointed the eyes of the blind man with the clay. And He said to him, "Go, wash in the pool of Siloam" (which is translated, Sent). So he went and washed, and came back seeing* (John 9:6-7).

In this, Jesus called on the man to believe and to obey in order to activate his faith. The blind man could have done several things other than go to the specific well Jesus indicated to clean off the mess left on his face. He could have gotten offended at

Jesus's method and walked away in a huff. But instead he obeyed the letter of Jesus's directions to him and *"came back seeing."*

On the other hand, neither did Jesus tell people, "Well, if you would just get your acts together and believe the Word of God given to you, then you would be healed. What's wrong with you?"[3] When He met ten lepers and they cried out to Him for mercy, He didn't heal them on the spot, but instead told them to do what was prescribed in the Law of Moses for lepers who had been cleansed as specified in Leviticus 14: *"Go, show yourselves to the priests."*[4] He didn't chide them for not having faith enough to take these Scriptures as their own promise to be healed, but instead came alongside them and taught them what they needed to know, mixing it with His own faith. The Bible then tells us, *"As they went, they were cleansed."*[5] Through sympathy and compassion, Jesus genuinely connected with these ten, feeling for them to the point of action, to the point of feeling the pain of their disease and doing what was within His power to do.

> *"Empathy makes us caring and vulnerable enough to sincerely connect with others, even in the worst of conditions, and love them."*

As Andrew Boyd, author and social activist, describes compassion:

> Compassion hurts. When you feel connected to everything, you also feel responsible for everything. And you cannot turn away. Your destiny is bound with the destinies of others. You must either learn to carry the Universe or be crushed by it. You must grow strong enough to love the world, yet empty enough to sit down at the same table with its worst horrors.

Jesus was willing to overcome the cultural stigma that looked upon lepers as outcasts, teach them what they needed to know to be healed, and send them on their way to receive healing by connecting with the word God had already sent them.

I once read that when William and Catherine Booth opened up soup kitchens and boarding places for the homeless in the streets of London, that they refused to offer food or lodging without asking that something was contributed in return, even if it was only a pittance. If they didn't even have a pittance to give, then they would be allowed to ply their trade to fix something, help sweep up, or perform another token of labor in exchange for a night's room and board.

Today we hear a great deal in the news about entitlement, abusing the system, cold-hearted politicians, and the like, but we hear very little about preserving the dignity of every individual, empowerment, or exercising true empathy to help in ways that don't hurt in the end. We could certainly take a lesson from Jesus, or even the Salvation Army, in how to reach out with a helping hand more effectively and genuinely connect with other people.

Prosperity Point

Empathy makes us caring and vulnerable enough to sincerely connect with others, even in the worst of conditions, and love them. It also goes the extra mile by sticking with them until they are back on their own two feet. It is much easier though to do *for* others than to take the time to work *with* them, whether our children, our spouse, someone at work, or someone we are volunteering to help. We need to engage with others in such a way that is both loving and empowering if we are to interact with them as Jesus would Himself.

Prosperity Thought

By this we know love, because He laid down His life for us. ...But whoever has this world's goods, and sees his brother in need, and shuts up his heart from him, how does the love of God abide in him?
(1 John 3:16-17)

Day Twenty-Two

FORGIVENESS

Forgive us our sins, as we have forgiven those who sin against us (Matthew 6:12 NLT).

The way most people talk about forgiveness today, you would think it didn't cost anything or take any effort at all. In our modern "I'm okay, you're okay" world that has grown a little bit tipsy on positive mental attitude messages, we seem to equate forgiveness with disregarding negative comments and overlooking that someone just cut us off on the freeway or took a little too long ordering coffee in the line ahead of us. While forgiveness is certainly those things, it is also something much deeper. It is not just the overlooking of slights; it is engaging with our deepest and darkest hurts to turn them over to the One Righteous Judge.

As beings created in the image of God, we have some of our Father's characteristics. One of those is the seeming paradoxical demand for both justice and mercy. When we are wronged, or we see someone else wronged, we sense the need for retribution—*"life for life, eye for eye, tooth for tooth, hand for hand, foot for foot, burn for burn, wound for wound, bruise for bruise."*[1] We understand that there is a very real cost to transgressing the laws of God and the universe. We also acknowledge that there is damage done when someone "hurts" us. It could be biting words, it could be being abused as a child, it could be being taken advantage of by a friend or colleague, or a broken promise in a marriage. It could be in our families, in our churches, or within our nations. It could be caused by simple neglect or from deep psychological wounds, racism, or bigotry.

Forgiveness is not just a matter of simply overlooking a wrong; it is a legal procedure in the Kingdom of Heaven. Someone has to pay for the wrong done. Recompense must be made. Forgiveness acknowledges that fact, but does so in a way that releases the offending person from being the one who suffers for it.

A good example of this is a story Shelley Hundley tells in her book *A Call for Justice.* Shelly grew up in a missionary compound in Columbia during some of its most violent years. Not only was life very difficult in this war zone, but Shelley was also sexually abused, something so horrific for her that she completely repressed the memories until she returned to the United States to attend college. While there, she became an outspoken atheist, but then also had a mental breakdown as the memories of what had happened to her as a child began to resurface. Only a very serious collision with God's love kept her from killing herself. As she described the conflict between forgiveness and justice:

> It is easy for well-meaning Christians to reduce forgiveness to sweeping transgression under the rug, but this becomes catastrophic in the face of life's most evil atrocities. How can we sweep sexual abuse under the rug? How can we tell someone whose heart has been crushed, "Move on, and don't let the offense steal your joy"?...
>
> Through forgiveness we release our case to a just Judge who will fight for us....
>
> Anyone can...tell a wounded person to "get over it," but that is not the answer that Christ brings. He reaches into the deepest places of our hearts and does a deep work of healing that allows us to forgive and even pray that those who wronged us will not have to experience God's fierce wrath.[2]

To forgive requires that we first and foremost recognize what it cost that we, ourselves, were forgiven. We recognize that the cross was a legal requirement for our being made right with God, and that its work is total and complete. To forgive is to acknowledge that the debt owed because of the wrongdoing has been paid in full and for all time.

It is easier to recognize this on the surface, however, than it is to live by it. Wrongs, hurts, and slights have a way of being passed over and not really forgiven. They then eat at us from the inside, creating bitterness that sinks its roots down into our souls, blocking the flow of our life energies and plugging the holes through which God whispers into our spiritual ears. Like rampant weeds, bitterness must be actively rooted out, or it can sour our outlook and poison the words that come from our mouth, eliciting the power of death in our words rather than the power of life.[3] When unforgiveness and bitterness have a chokehold on our souls, true prosperity is impossible.

"To forgive requires that we first and foremost recognize what it cost that we, ourselves, were forgiven."

In Matthew 18:21-22, Peter came to Jesus with a very provocative question about forgiveness. Peter asked:

> *"Lord, how often shall my brother sin against me, and I forgive him? Up to seven times?" Jesus said to him, "I do not say to you, up to seven times, but up to seventy times seven."*

Forgiveness is not necessarily a one-time event. You will likely have to repeatedly forgive a person who has wounded you.

The first few times you do this may *feel* hypocritical, but forgiveness is not a *feeling*. It is an act of your will. As you consistently choose to forgive instead of keeping those negative emotions alive, you will find your anger and hatred begin to subside. Keep in mind that forgiveness does not mean you totally dismiss or condone wrong and hurtful behavior. It simply means you no longer seek to get even or to punish your offender. It means you're able to pray that God will bless him or her and truly mean it. As author and theologian Lewis Smedes wrote, "To forgive is to set a prisoner free and discover that the prisoner was you."

The late South African President Nelson Mandela was challenged to forgive those who persecuted him. After spending more than twenty-seven years in prison for his anti-apartheid activism, he saw apartheid come to an end and eventually became the nation's first black president. At his inauguration, Mandela invited the warden of the prison—where he'd spent so many years—to sit with him front and center. As journalist Deroy Murdock observed, "While most people would be tempted to lock up their jailers if they had the chance, Mandela essentially forgave him while the whole world and his own people, white and black, were watching."

"Resentment," Mandela once said, "is like drinking poison and then hoping it will kill your enemies."

The true work of forgiveness happens when you take your offender before the Judge of Heaven and earth in prayer. It means you must stand behind the prosecution table and state your case, acknowledging what happened to you—the damage done—and then ask for recompense. You must ask your heavenly Advocate for damages to be repaid, for injuries to be healed, for wrongs done you to be righted. When you finally look over to the defendant's table, however, you need to see that it is no longer the accused who hurt you sitting there, but Jesus Himself. It is Jesus, because He is the One who paid for the offender's wrongs, and it is He alone who can heal hurts, repair damages, and right wrongs. When you're able to see that, then you can forgive. You can release whatever happened to you into God's capable hands and ask for mercy for the other person.

> ***Forgiveness releases us from the bonds of bitterness that can poison our souls.***

Justice is satisfied through Jesus's sacrifice on the cross. It is justice that allows Him to forgive us—*"If we confess our sins, He is faithful and just to forgive us our sins and to cleanse us from all unrighteousness"*[4]—and that allows us to embrace those we would accuse and look to God for recompense instead. It allows you and me to call for God's justice in the life of the other person. And that frees us to release what was done to us and move on with our lives.

That is not always an easy process. Sometimes we have to take our hurts to the judgment throne of God more than once. Emotions will try to drag justice back into our own hands, but we must keep repeating to ourselves, "I gave that to God. I don't have it anymore. I have forgiven that person." Then we can let God make up the difference for whatever was lost and heal whatever was wounded.

Prosperity Point

The road to freedom is paved by forgiveness. Author and speaker Dr. Judith Orloff describes this process as follows:

> Forgiveness is a paradigm-shifting solution for transforming anger. It liberates you from the trap of endless revenge so that you can experience more joy and connection. Forgiveness does more for you than anyone else because it liberates you from negativity and lets you move forward. Forgiving might not make anger totally dissolve, but it will give you the freedom of knowing you are so much more.[5]

It is forgiveness that frees us of the *"weight, and the sin which so easily ensnares us."*[6] More than those who have offended or harmed us, forgiveness releases us from the bonds of bitterness that can poison our souls.

Leave things in the hands of the true and righteous Judge who looks out for us and to whom vengeance alone belongs. Then move on as best you can until your full healing and restoration comes from that same righteous Source.

Prosperity Thought

I suppose that since most of our hurts come through relationships so will our healing, and I know that grace rarely makes sense for those looking in from the outside.

—William P. Young,
The Shack

Day Twenty-Three

KINDNESS

Let all bitterness, wrath, anger, clamor, and evil speaking be put away from you, with all malice. And be kind to one another, tenderhearted, forgiving one another, even as God in Christ forgave you (Ephesians 4:31-32).

In 2 Samuel 9, we find David established as king over the entire land of Israel. He had returned the Ark of the Covenant to the tabernacle in Jerusalem, rejoined Judah and Israel as one people, and defeated all of Israel's enemies in the surrounding territories. For the first time in too long to remember, David was at peace. He started looking for some good to do.

Remembering his deep brotherly love for his friend Jonathan, the son of Saul, he asked his advisors, *"Is there still anyone who is left of the house of Saul, that I may show him kindness for Jonathan's sake?"*[1]

It turned out that there was. Jonathan had a son named Mephibosheth who was probably the last living heir of King Saul. There was a bit of a problem, though. Mephibosheth was in hiding. As far as he was concerned, David was after his life.

You see, when Mephibosheth was young and it was heard that Saul and Jonathan were dead in battle, his nurse took young Mephibosheth up in her arms and ran, thinking that at any minute David or his representatives would storm Jerusalem and slaughter any remaining descendants of Saul in order to eliminate their claim on the throne. In her rush, she tripped and fell.

Mephibosheth was injured so badly that he was left lame. Since then he had grown into a young man, hiding all the while in the barren country near Lo Debar. There was good evidence to support that Mephibosheth grew up fearing David, and perhaps even despising him for taking the throne that really should have come down to him.

None of this mattered to David, though. David and Mephibosheth's father had been best friends, and since Jonathan was no longer alive for David to bless, he wanted to bless the closest person to his friend he could find. That meant Mephibosheth. David was excited to hear that he was alive and called for him to be brought to Jerusalem at once.

When Mephibosheth entered into David's throne room, David cried out at once, "Mephibosheth!"

Mephibosheth crumbled to the ground before him. "Here is your servant!" he answered.

David must have all but waved away Mephibosheth's shame and fear. Having him lifted to his feet, he told him, *"Do not fear, for I will surely show you kindness for Jonathan your father's sake, and will restore to you all the land of Saul your grandfather; and you shall eat bread at my table continually."*[2]

David showed kindness to Mephibosheth for the sake of Jonathan. And that is what kindness is really all about.

To be kind is much more than being nice to other people. Kindness is rooted in relationship. David's kindness to Mephibosheth was rooted in David's relationship with Jonathan. It had nothing to do with what Mephibosheth deserved, nothing to do with what Mephibosheth thought of David, and nothing to do with anything David wanted from Mephibosheth. It was born out of the fact that David had been blessed by God to be where he was at that time and it made him want to find someone he could bless in a similar way.

Kindness is a general disposition to bless others that comes out of our strength, faithfulness, and love for God. We can't really understand kindness apart from all three of these terms. Kindness requires strength, because it is difficult to bless others if we are not in a good, solid place ourselves; it requires faithfulness, because kindness is not always reciprocated—it requires a proactiveness that disposes with any attitudes reflecting a "what's in it for me" attitude; and it requires love, because kindness is one of the truest expressions of the unconditional, God-kind-of-love.

In fact, kindness is one of the truest expressions of the character of God. We see it in the life of Jesus from His interactions with little children to healing the sick and disabled to teaching the people about the true nature of the Kingdom. We even see the confrontive kindness He used to call out the religious leaders of the day, trying to shock their sense of self-righteousness enough to draw them back to God. We see it when He cleansed the temple of money changers and when He cleared a house of mourners to raise a dead girl back to life. With kindness, Jesus expressed both the power and the tenderness of the Father.

> *Kindness is one of the truest expressions of the character of God.*

We underestimate kindness if we see it as anything other than one of the most powerful tools of Kingdom expansion. Kindness is a proactive force we should never underestimate. It should be a general expression from us toward the people whom God loves, for the sake of our own relationship with God.

At the same time, we should remember that kindness isn't to be reserved for people we've just met. In many ways, being kind to strangers is easier than to people we have history with. True kindness, however, is based in relationship. Had David had the option, he would have gladly blessed his friend Jonathan rather than Jonathan's son. David and Jonathan had gone so far as to establish a covenant partnership, dedicating everything each had to the welfare of the other. This type of covenant regard was often referred to as "loving-kindness."

This being true, how can a husband and wife—the deepest form of covenant partnership—be unkind to one another? How can we be kinder to people we hardly know than we are to those we are closest with? Is the kindness we show a stranger really worth anything if we're unable to show loving-kindness to those we interact with most?

This is why kindness can't be sentimentalized. It is not based in feeling, but in strength, faithfulness and dedication, and in unconditional love. It demands that we be in a good place with God ourselves—a strong place, a dedicated place, a loved place—so that we can express genuine kindness to others. If we can do that, Kingdom living will radically change the world we live in.

Prosperity Point

Kindness is the *modus operandi* of the Kingdom of Heaven. It is where the love of God meets the rough reality of the world that can at times be incredibly cruel, manipulative, selfish, and unfair. Kindness is anchored on the sacrifice Jesus offered on the cross, the covenant of forgiveness He established with His own blood, and the Kingdom of His followers He came back from the dead to create. As you walk throughout your day, remember the kindness of Jesus toward you. For His sake, extend that kindness to others.

Prosperity Thought

Guard well within yourself that treasure, kindness. Know how to give without hesitation, how to lose without regret, how to acquire without meanness.

—George Sand

Day Twenty-Four

GOODNESS

Love from the center of who you are; don't fake it. Run for dear life from evil; hold on for dear life to good (Romans 12:9 MSG).

One of the most vile things plaguing our culture today—even in the Church—is cynicism. This means, by definition, that we don't trust the motives and capacity for good in other people. This is an insidious plague, and often runs so deeply within us that we don't notice it is there. It poisons the very air that we breathe, and every thought we think. Though we talk at great lengths about what we want to do and how we want to help others, ultimately cynicism ties our hands from doing much of anything significant, because, underneath it all, we just don't believe it will do any good.

Cynicism is what makes us look away from the homeless person panhandling on the street corner, makes the young person look at the old in their church as clueless rather than filled with experience and wisdom, hardens the hearts of the older generation to the young because "these kids just don't listen today," makes us give up on loved ones because we start to believe the lie that "they're never going to change," turns our workplaces into arenas of competition rather than cooperation, and basically makes us distrustful and pessimistic. Many times we successfully cover this with a good attitude, a bright smiling face, and an outgoing personality, but until we delve into our hearts to dig cynicism out at its root, our effectiveness as ambassadors of Christ will be hindered.

This subliminal distrust of others sinks into our minds and acts to justify our own selfishness and "looking out for number one." It encourages us to guard our turf rather than risk our efforts or assets to invest in others. It distances us from those with characteristics that "rub us the wrong way," makes us believe we can't depend on someone, or convinces us that they are just trying to take advantage of us in some way, shape, or form. We become convinced that they don't "contribute" to their employer, society, or even their own families enough to warrant our efforts to help them to better themselves. It is cynicism that strangles empathy and turns it into a legalistic, condemning attitude.

"The only cure for eliminating cynicism is to replace it with goodness tempered by wisdom."

Cynicism rises out of experience. None of us have gone through life without someone disappointing us, hurting us, or taking something we offered freely and failing to appreciate it as we think they should. They have "wasted" our efforts, so why should we risk doing anything more on their behalf?

Now, I am not saying that we don't have to manage our time and assets to try to maximize our "return on investment," but what I am saying is 1) we have to root cynicism out of our souls because it blocks the work of God flowing out of our hearts, and 2) our job is not always to "maximize return"—that should be God's blessing. Our job is to obey His dictates and commandments. The only real cure for eliminating cynicism deep down in our hearts is to replace it with goodness that is tempered by wisdom. Regarding this, Jesus gave this admonition:

> *Stay alert. This is hazardous work I'm assigning you. You're going to be like sheep running through a wolf pack, so don't call attention to yourselves. Be as cunning as a snake, inoffensive as a dove* (Matthew 10:16 MSG).

He was saying that we will run into great challenges in life—like a single sheep surrounded by our wolves—but, assignments from Him are what we should focus on, not on the dangers, defeats, or circumstances. We should ask Him for wisdom and live by His cunning—but that cunning is not to promote ourselves over others. We are instead to be pure of motive and as harmless as a dove.

Perhaps the best example of this is again the sower Jesus spoke of in Mark 4, whom we spoke of earlier. From the outside, this farmer seemed rather foolish, as he didn't regard the ground in which he "invested" his seed before he tossed it there. In fact, it was as if he were blind to the different type of soils where he was throwing his seed. He certainly had more confidence in his seed than he did regard for the soil where he hoped it would take root and grow. And, in a sense, he was simply obedient to the will of his Storyteller, who made him the hero of the parable.

"Good works must flow out of the goodness of God overflowing the banks of our souls."

In a similar way, we are to sow goodness into our world out of the goodness—the grace—overflowing from our hearts. We are not supposed to worry about the results of our actions as much as we are to be loyal and obedient to our callings—we leave the results, the germination of the seed that sprouts up and blooms, in the hands of God. Our job is to sow and water and nurture, it is God who brings the increase. As Paul prayed for the Thessalonians:

> *Therefore we also pray always for you that our God would count you worthy of this calling, and fulfill all the good pleasure of His goodness and the work of faith with power, that the name of our Lord Jesus Christ may be glorified in you, and you in Him, according to the grace of our God and the Lord Jesus Christ* (2 Thessalonians 1:11-12).

In the late 1990s, management guru Peter Drucker described the Salvation Army as "the most effective organization in the United States." What they did with so little to help so many truly amazed him. One of the primary keys that he spoke of in relation to this was that the organization was not functioning simply as a charity. He saw them as people who truly invested in others with a very real expectation of positive returns. As he put it:

> Yes, you have some charitable operations, some soup kitchens and so forth. But they are a fairly small part of your programs. A major part of your efforts is in rehabilitation. And that is pure venture capitalism. Your investment in people gets incredible returns.[1]

In this light, the sower was a venture capitalist of the most reckless nature, and I believe so is God. After all, He "sowed" His own Son to invest in this earth for the sake of reaping a harvest that includes you and me! What a risk! What could He have possibly been thinking? But He did it, because He knew the return on that investment would be worth it. And I, for one, want to make sure He was right.

Prosperity Point

Good works must flow out of the goodness of God overflowing the banks of our souls. If they do not, then they are simply whitewash on the outside of a sepulcher, a place that may look pristine, but inside is filled with death. We must guard our motives and be sure we act with purity of love and confidence in the efforts, words, and time we invest. We must let our cynicism be replaced with God's goodness within us, and then cultivate it until it can't help but pour out of us to others. That is the *"goodness of God* [that] *leads...to repentance."*[2]

Prosperity Thought

Do your little bit of good where you are; it's those little bits of good put together that overwhelm the world.
—Desmond Tutu

Day Twenty-Five

AGREEMENT

Take this most seriously: A yes on earth is yes in heaven; a no on earth is no in heaven. What you say to one another is eternal. I mean this. When two of you get together on anything at all on earth and make a prayer of it, my Father in heaven goes into action. And when two or three of you are together because of me, you can be sure that I'll be there (Matthew 18:18-20 MSG).

There are three places in the Scriptures where the Bible tells us God will get so involved in something that He will *"command the blessing."* The first two are on our storehouses, which we will discuss in the last week on financial prosperity. The other is on being in unity:

> *Behold, how good and how pleasant it is for brethren to dwell together in unity! ...For there the Lord commanded the blessing—life forevermore* (Psalm 133:1,3).

In the book of Matthew, Jesus simplifies this principle even further, telling us it is not necessarily about an entire community or congregation coming together in agreement, but even if just two or three are gathered in His name, He will be there; and if those two or three agree—really get on the same page and agree—about something in prayer, God will go into action to accomplish it. Look at how those verses, Matthew 18:19-20, read in the New King James Version of the Bible:

> *I say to you that if two of you agree on earth concerning anything that they ask, it will be done for them by My Father in heaven. For where two or three are gathered together in My name, I am there in the midst of them.*

But how few of us live in that reality?

The operative word in this passage is *agree.* When Jesus used this word, I don't believe He was thinking of two people *agreeing* to have lunch together. I don't think He was talking about the type of unity where people come together over a few common interests to stand for something that is more about compromise than truth. I don't believe that there was anything casual or transient about the agreement Jesus meant here. I believe He was talking about two or three coming together to settle a matter together once and for all, whether that be ending the sale of drugs in their neighborhood, someone receiving healing for an illness, or light being shown on human trafficking so its victims could be rescued and delivered. This agreement is the bonding together of two hearts for or against something, issuing a "yes" or "no" on the earth that will resound in the halls of Heaven.

"Agreement is the bonding together of two hearts for or against something, issuing a "yes" or "no" on the earth that will resound in the halls of Heaven."

It is such agreement—such unity of heart—that is the essence of the Kingdom of God. The Kingdom of God, after all, is about joining together, where the kingdom of darkness is about dividing apart. If possible, the enemy will even turn our soul against our spirit, making us double-minded, deafening our spiritual ears, and blinding us to our own selfishness. It will divide brother against brother, sister against sister, and child against parent. Why? Because true unity—that which harnesses the force of agreement—is power for transformation.

This is why God seeks intimacy—"into-me-see"—with us. It is why there is a need within us to be known—fully known, if possible—and loved. Why? Because the closer our bond, the more intimate we are with one another, the more we walk in agreement, and the greater our influence in Heaven. As best-selling author Elizabeth Gilbert said, "To be fully seen by somebody... and be loved anyhow—this is a human offering that can border on miraculous." If she only knew it didn't just *border* on miraculous, it pressed fully into it!

Now a lot of people mistake being involved sexually with someone as being intimate with them. There is some truth to this, but it is just on the surface. To share physical "intimacy" is not very difficult, but to share each other's hearts, that is no small matter—and a lot more risky. It requires the bearing of one's soul. It requires real trust, because when you open up your heart to another it makes you vulnerable. It means talking about more than surface issues. It means we have to be willing to pay the price necessary to help the other person become whole and fulfilled in his or her own callings. It is a level of covenant agreement that says, "We pledge our energy, our resources, and our determination that this matter is settled before the court of God." This is the type of prayer that really activates Heaven.

> *"True wealth is the quality of our relationships and the influence we have to help others live the best lives they can."*

If we are going to operate in this kind of power in prayer, we have to learn to develop this kind of unity and agreement with others. We have to learn what it really means to "join forces" to address whatever it is that moves us to pray. We have to be trusting brothers and sisters willing to see beyond the slights, offenses, and competitiveness that so often divides us into factions within our families, our churches, our communities, and our nations. We need to come into oneness with Christ so that there is room for us to be one with each other.

This is the "agreement" Jesus spoke of in Matthew 18. Think about it for a moment. If we could *agree* in this way, would anything be able to stand against us?

PROSPERITY POINT

The Kingdom of God creates unity, oneness, and wholeness; the kingdom of darkness divides, segregates, contends, and corrupts. As James wrote, *"If you have bitter envy and self-seeking in your hearts, do not boast and lie against the truth. ...For where envy and self-seeking exist, confusion and every evil thing are there."*[1] Agreement doesn't happen until we can stand for each other as much as we stand for ourselves.

Never forget that true wealth is the quality of our relationships and the influence we have to help others live the best lives they can. We can't come into agreement without a degree of transparency and honesty that allows us to confess our faults to one another and to forgive. That means we must be trustworthy enough for others to be vulnerable in front of us and know that we will not use that vulnerability against them later. It is why there is power in confessing our mistakes and weaknesses to one another, as James advised, *"Confess your trespasses to one another, and pray for one another, that you may be healed."*[2] This is the place of unity and agreement, and when it happens, Heaven will move earth to accomplish what we pray for.

PROSPERITY THOUGHT

Then I will give them a heart to know Me, that I am the Lord; and they shall be My people, and I will be their God, for they shall return to Me with their whole heart (Jeremiah 24:7).

Week Six

SOCIAL PROSPERITY

You are not here merely to make a living. You are here in order to enable the world to live more amply, with greater vision, with a finer spirit of hope and achievement. You are here to enrich the world, and you impoverish yourself if you forget the errand.

—Woodrow Wilson

Day Twenty-Six

INTEGRITY

To sell your soul is the easiest thing in the world. That's what everybody does every hour of his life. If I asked you to keep your soul—would you understand why that's much harder?

—Ayn Rand,

The Fountainhead

"Good" is quite often the enemy of "best." Romans 12:2 tells us to *"not be conformed to this world, but be transformed by the renewing of your mind, that you may prove what is that good and acceptable and perfect will of God."* If you had a choice, which would you prefer to be in: the "good," "acceptable," or "perfect" will of God?

I have always found this process to be somewhat progressive. We have a choice, as we pursue God's purpose for our lives, to move through all three of these levels of God's calling for us, or to settle back and be complacent about where God wants us. As new Christians, we come into a good place with God, right with Him again because we have accepted Jesus's sacrifice on our behalf, have acknowledged that He was raised from the dead, and have invited Him to be the Lord of our lives. In so doing, we have asked Him to be our guide and direct our steps. At first, it is simple obedience to His Word and the principles of His teachings. Then it is recognizing certain dispositions in ourselves that give us clues as to what God wants to do through our lives. Then, ultimately, God draws us closer into partnership with Him. We move deeper and deeper into His will for our lives, seeking to live a life that is ultimately *"in step with the Spirit."*[1] But this last phase doesn't happen just because we sign up.

Most of us wander around in the outer court of the "acceptable" will of God, living in the benefits of fellowship and the promise that we will one day be with our Lord in Heaven, but not quite satisfied with the life we have. Many of us are good at acting the part of the happy Christian, but as U2 sings it, we "still haven't found what we're looking for." We are doing something very closely akin to the life God wants for us, something that runs parallel and in tandem with it, but it is still a half step removed—and deep in our souls we sense it.

Why do we hold back from stepping into the *perfect* will of God? Because we know there is a cost. It will demand going beyond our comfort zone. It might mean taking a risk—a leap of faith to act on an idea. It might mean starting something completely new. It might mean change. Sacrifice. Getting up an hour or two earlier to write or blog, or volunteering after work to speak out or take a stand on a social or political issue. In whatever arena God is drawing your heart, it is a bigger playing field—the Big Games—where you go for gold instead of settling for silver or bronze, or worse, just make a showing.

"To live with integrity is to live with purity of motive and purpose."

To live with integrity is to live with purity of motive and purpose. Integrity is often used to describe the strength of metal or steel—that it has a certain quality—and that it is unified, unimpaired, or sound in construction. To speak of the integrity of a recording means there is no background noise to interfere with the quality of what is being played, spoken, or sung. It is to capture the essence of the message without distraction or dilution. It is to clear away the things that would distract us from focusing on the perfect will of God—to refuse compromise when it comes to our own conduct. It is to go boldly and bravely into the throne room of God and ask Him what He really wants of us.

To live in integrity is to pursue living in God's best for us. This doesn't necessarily mean opulence in material goods, but rather opulence in finding fulfillment in life, wholeheartedly pursuing the solution to whatever mystery God has placed before us, whatever community we need to reach with His love, or whatever issue He has called us to address. It means living in the rhythm of grace so that we have overflow of energy, confidence, and care for our family, friends, colleagues, and those we encounter throughout our days. One thing we must do with integrity, where we must not compromise, is in being filled up with the Spirit of God each day and having excess to pour out on others.

Integrity is foundational for every relationship in your life. Can you be trusted to tell the truth? To do what you say you are going to do? To have your words based in truth rather than hype? To have the other person's best interests at heart rather than just your own? The degrees of difference between these can be very small—as is the difference between living in the "good" or "acceptable" will of God versus His perfect will.

One of the most difficult things about integrity is that it takes time for it to be noticed. There are a lot of people out there who can playact at having integrity and they are so good at it that it is hard to tell it from the real thing. However, it becomes obvious over time. It is recognized when, encounter after encounter, people find you to be a person who will do what is right, even if it is not in your own best interest. Integrity must be a lifestyle. It must be lived as outlined in Proverbs 3:3-4:

> *Do not let kindness and truth leave you; bind them around your neck, write them on the tablet of your heart. So you will find favor and good repute in the sight of God and man* (NASB).

Prosperity Point

Integrity is the pursuit of living honestly, transparently, and purposefully. It is to value the trust of others above your own promotion or benefit, and a dedication to truth above simply having something clever to say. It must be a foundational principle upon which you build every relationship in your life, and it must be communicated with confidence, kindness, and regard to genuinely connecting with what is happening in the lives of others. It means having an uncompromising dedication to experiencing God's best in your life and in the lives of those you interact with.

Prosperity Thought

Remember, we Christians think man lives forever. Therefore, what really matters is those little marks or twists on the central, inside part of the soul which are going to turn it, in the long run, into a heavenly or a hellish creature.

—C.S. Lewis,
Mere Christianity

Day Twenty-Seven

KINGDOM-MINDEDNESS

Your kingdom come. Your will be done,
on earth as it is in heaven
(Matthew 6:10).

I teach a great deal about how we manifest the Kingdom of God in my courses, books, and seminars, because it is so central to our mission on this earth as Christians. Jesus made it rather plain, after all, that the primary key to accessing the prosperity of Heaven is to *"seek the Kingdom of God above all else, and live righteously, and He will give you everything you need."*[1]

When we ask that God's will be done on earth in the same way it is in Heaven, we are asking that things on earth be administrated in the same way they are administrated in Heaven. We are inviting the government of God into our families, our churches, our workplaces, communities, and our nations. We are inviting the government of Heaven to pervade our streets, homes, and institutions. We invite His efficiency, His expertise, His care, His attention to detail, His innovation, and His perseverance into our lives, and thus into everywhere we go. We also invite His purposes, His grace, and His answers.

Think, for example, how a hospital in our fallen world would function if Heaven were in charge of its administration. Yes, certainly more healing would be available, but what about all of the daily functions required to care for the sick and injured? What would the interactions between the doctors, nurses, and other staff members be like? What would the same look like at the DMV? In your police station? Where you work? Even in your church?

We too often forget that we are called to be the same Kingdom-minded people at work Monday through Friday as we are at church. The Kingdom of God cannot be pigeonholed into Sunday mornings, Wednesday nights, or whenever we might happen to be around other believers. We must be filled to overflowing so it sloshes out of us in every interaction and encounter of our day. It should be contagious, it should be viral, and if it isn't, what exactly is going wrong?

Look for a moment at how Jesus referred to the Kingdom of Heaven:

- As a grain of mustard seed—though it may start as the smallest of all seeds, when it grows, it becomes a place of shelter, lodging, and protection.[2]
- As leaven—just a little bit of it will go a long way. If you add it to a lump of dough, it will permeate the lump and affect everything it comes into contact with.[3]
- As a treasure hidden in a field and a pearl of great price—it is worth selling everything we own to possess it.[4] In fact, if we don't trust in the Kingdom more than our material blessings, it will be hard for us to enter it at all.[5]
- As a net thrown into the sea—when we cast it as instructed, it will fill with every kind of fish.[6]
- As a man hiring workers for his vineyard and a king inviting guests to his son's wedding—those who answer the invitation will receive their reward whether they come early or late, and while all are

invited, it is up to us to RSVP: *"For many are called, but few are chosen."*[7]

All of these metaphors serve to teach us about the value and nature of the Kingdom of God. Reading these, there is no question that Jesus believed that this Kingdom would spread like wildfire if we would but demonstrate it to others as He did. And I am not just talking about performing miracles and healing the sick or infirm, I am talking about spreading it in every action, word, and attitude in every interaction and encounter. It is about being a blessing, whether that be sharing a word of wisdom, praying for someone, or just being with them and loving them as they suffer through something.

"We should simply present Jesus as He is—as He has shown Himself to be in our own lives."

Paul went so far as to call us God's representatives—His ambassadors—from the Kingdom of Heaven to the earth:

> *So we are Christ's ambassadors, God making His appeal as it were through us. We [as Christ's personal representatives] beg you for His sake to lay hold of the divine favor [now offered you] and be reconciled to God* (2 Corinthians 5:20 AMP).

As Christ's ambassadors, we are to hold forth the work He did on the cross, reconciling the world to God. We are to offer it so that they can accept it, purchasing it as a pearl of great price by investing their very lives and ambitions in it. And it shouldn't come through twisting their arms or manipulating their emotions. We should simply present Jesus as He is—as He has shown Himself to be in our own lives. Testifying of His love, goodness, and faithfulness will infect them with Kingdom "leaven" that will begin to permeate their thoughts and actions.

Prosperity Point

We are ambassadors of the Kingdom of God—representatives in a foreign and strange place that doesn't understand the wonders or fulfillment that comes with being a citizen of Heaven. Scripture tells us, *"The kingdom of God is within you."*[8] If we are wall-to-wall Kingdom of God on the inside, then we shouldn't have to do much to let it out. It shouldn't be a hard sell to others; it should be evident in everything we do and say.

Prosperity Thought

The way we are with each other is the truest test of our faith. How I treat a brother or sister from day to day, how I react to the sin-scarred wino on the street, how I respond to interruptions from people I dislike, how I deal with normal people in their normal confusion on a normal day may be a better indication of my reverence for life than the antiabortion sticker on the bumper of my car.

—Brennan Manning,
The Ragamuffin Gospel

Day Twenty-Eight

LEADERSHIP

Leadership is not about titles, positions, or flowcharts.
It is about one life influencing another.
—John C. Maxwell

The Lincoln Memorial in our nation's capital is a grand monument not just honoring a president, but also symbolizing a catalyst of change. Lincoln was a courageous trailblazer who, in a unique moment of history, altered the course of a nation's destiny. In so doing, he helped the world to understand that everyone can find value in the process of embracing, promoting, and establishing social justice by claiming the virtues of equality and dignity.

Today, our world is suffering from a vacuum of such bold, moral leadership. Robert McDonald, CEO and President of Proctor & Gamble, put it this way, "Leadership is the scarcest resource, and the most important resource, in the world. Nothing happens without leadership." Every country, government, business, and organization requires leadership. Whenever you see a successful company, institution, ministry, or nation, you will find at the forefront an effective leader. From Chrysler to AOL, from Delta Airlines to McDonald's, from worship to warfare, from playground to playhouse to God's house of prayer, success can be found in one single element—effective leadership. I believe that a leader is the most valuable person in society. No cause or goal can be accomplished without a leader.

Leaders are frontline individuals. They are industry risk takers, trailblazers, revolutionaries, and agents of change. They are thinkers, tinkerers, inventors, and innovators. They are single mothers who raise upright citizens. They are young people who refuse to bow to peer pressure, but instead live counterculturally. They are those who push envelopes, live on the edge, and while championing a cause, successfully motivate others to follow. John Quincy Adams said, "If your actions inspire others to dream more, learn more, do more, and become more, you are a leader." Leaders are not always those who do the big out-front things. They are individuals who do small things in big ways.

Scripture makes plain that if you are faithful in small things, those things will grow. Everything starts as a seed, even the Kingdom of Heaven.[1] Yesterday we talked about the transformative power of a little leaven. Likewise, we read in Luke that, *"If you are faithful in little things, you will be faithful in large ones. But if you are dishonest in little things, you won't be honest with greater responsibilities."*[2] We are told that even Jesus Himself started His mission in relative obscurity, as little by little, from a child, *"Jesus increased in wisdom and stature, and in favor with God and men."*[3]

> *No cause or goal can be accomplished without a leader.*

When Nehemiah began to rebuild the walls of Jerusalem, there were only a few people with him. The Lord asked:

> *The hands of Zerubbabel have laid the foundation of this temple; his hands shall also finish it. ...For who has despised the day of small things?* (Zechariah 4:9-10)

Why? Because he who despises starting at the bottom and growing—working his way up—will never be a great leader. Only those who know how to follow, how to obey in the little things, paying attention to *all* of the details, will know how to handle all of the demands of leading many in a larger organization. Jesus illustrated this when He was asked, “Who will be the greatest in the Kingdom of Heaven?” In response:

> *Jesus called a little child to Him, set him in the midst of them, and said, “Assuredly, I say to you, unless you are converted and become as little children, you will by no means enter the kingdom of heaven. Therefore whoever humbles himself as this little child is the greatest in the kingdom of heaven”* (Matthew 18:2-4).

Notice what Jesus did. He called a child to Him. Now that child could have been playing a game with friends, running through the courtyard on an important errand, or even sitting at the outskirts of the small crowd straining to see what was going on. No matter, when he heard Jesus’s voice, he obeyed. Notice it is that act—doing just as this little child did—that Jesus commends as the key to being the *greatest* in the Kingdom of Heaven: *“Therefore whoever humbles himself as this little child is the greatest in the kingdom of heaven.”*

> *“Creating a successful strategy for leading ourselves enables us to see clearly enough to inspire and help others do the same.”*

“This little child” had no authority, but he did exert leadership influence—the most difficult kind, in fact—he showed the power of *self-leadership.* He showed that he was in charge of his own actions—an incredible sort of freedom, really—and could obey, even when there were likely other things he wanted to be doing. He was able to put his own needs and desires aside and obey what Jesus asked him to do. We must discipline ourselves accordingly and live in obedience to love at all times. As Eleanor Roosevelt put it, “To handle yourself, use your head; to handle others, use your heart.”

Until we can effectively lead ourselves, we will not be able to effectively lead others.

The best leaders rise not because of a hunger for authority or a need to prove they are capable, but by being effective influencers others will look to for motivation, encouragement, inspiration, and organization. You don't have to be the boss to have a good idea and the skills to bring it to fruition. In fact, the best place to start to lead is by taking care of the little things in your sphere of influence and doing them well. If we do those things with integrity and diligence, don't we prove we are capable of handling greater authority? As Jesus said, *"If you're not honest in small jobs, who will put you in charge of the store?"*[4]

I also like how Lao Tzu summed up the qualities of a good leader:

> I have three precious things which I hold fast and prize. The first is gentleness; the second is frugality; the third is humility, which keeps me from putting myself before others. Be gentle and you can be bold; be frugal and you can be liberal; avoid putting yourself before others and you can become a leader among men.

Creating a successful strategy for leading ourselves enables us to see clearly enough to inspire and help others do the same. That is influence; that is leadership. It is a mustard seed of leadership, to be sure, but then we know what mustard seeds do if we plant them and nurture them properly.

Prosperity Point

The ability to lead others starts with your ability to lead yourself, then the ability to be a leader in a small group, team, or in your family, then being a leader in an organization, in your community, then in the larger society. Each different level has its own tests and challenges, but the basic foundation you build as a person able to lead yourself by the direction of the Holy Spirit will serve you well at every level. Don't expect promotion until you prove you are confident and able to prosper right where you are at this moment. Certainly it can feel like oyur efforts are going unnoticed much of the time, but remember:

> *For not from the east nor from the west nor from the south come promotion and lifting up. But God is the Judge! He puts down one and lifts up another* (Psalm 75:6-7 AMP).

Allow your leadership—your influence—to emerge from following and obeying the Spirit of God. If that is how to be the greatest in the Kingdom of Heaven, it is also sure to help you in every other arena!

Prosperity Thought

A leader...is like a shepherd. He stays behind the flock, letting the most nimble go out ahead, whereupon the others follow, not realizing that all along they are being directed from behind.
—Nelson Mandela,
Long Walk to Freedom

Day Twenty-Nine

SERVICE

As each one has received a special gift, employ it in serving one another as good stewards of the manifold grace of God
(1 Peter 4:10 NASB).

First Peter 4:10 tells us that we have each been given special gifts and talents that are necessary to serve one another as God wants us to do. It also tells us that doing this shows good stewardship, or trusteeship, of the *"manifold grace of God." Manifold* literally means, "many folds or with many facets." Having many facets makes a diamond shine and catches the eye of other people. These facets release the beauty of the stone. Many would never recognize a diamond had it not been cut and these facets exposed.

Thus it is in service that we exercise our gifts rather than leaving them to atrophy from lack of use. Our gifts then grow, develop, and mature, fueled by grace. If we make no demand on grace to aid us in service, how do we stir it up in our lives? Imagine what the world would be like if the Church realized that one of the most important keys to drawing more of God's grace into the earth was to exercise our gifts and talents in service to one another.

Now, if we really want to activate grace in our lives, we once again can't be fragmenting who we are into a dozen different commitments and "personalities." We can't be one way in church, another when we volunteer at our kids' school, another at home, another working for a local charity, and yet a different person at work. Service must be a natural expression of who we are, wherever we are. Thus we should be the same "loving, Christianly servant" on our jobs as we are volunteering in the community. Certainly we may need to be more respectful of the beliefs of others in a place where there are fewer Christians, but the light inside of us should be shining no dimmer. The truth is, where there is more darkness and oppression, the more we should release the fragrance of the fruit of the Spirit. The sweet aroma of our sacrifice should be as present in "rehabilitating" a grouchy boss as much as in our efforts to rehabilitate a person with substance abuse problems. Service isn't just something we do for "service organizations," but everywhere we go.

On the other hand, it is not enough to just serve in places we routinely go. We need to get out of our comfort zones and look for opportunities to serve those who need it the most. We must seek out those Jesus called *"the least of these,"* because in so doing, we serve Him.

> *Then the King will say to those on His right hand, "Come, you blessed of My Father, inherit the kingdom prepared for you from the foundation of the world: for I was hungry and you gave Me food; I was thirsty and you gave Me drink; I was a stranger and you took Me in; I was naked and you clothed Me; I was sick and you visited Me; I was in prison and you came to Me."*
>
> *Then the righteous will answer Him, saying, "Lord, when did we see You hungry and feed You, or thirsty and give You drink? When did we see You a stranger and take You in, or naked and clothe You? Or when did we see You sick, or in prison, and come to You?" And the King will answer and say to them, "Assuredly, I say to you, inasmuch as you did it to one of the least of these My brethren, you did it to Me"* (Matthew 25:34-40).

To serve those who have no way to repay is to emulate God Himself. After all, what could we ever do to earn what He has done for us? Nothing. But we can love Him back by laying down our lives for others as He did—for the joy set before Him is the same joy He sets before us.

Oswald Chambers wrote, "To serve God is the deliberate love-gift of a nature that has heard the call of God."[1] Our service is the expression of who we are, of the "special gift" of God given to us in His calling. Though it is wonderful to serve because there is a need, there is another level of service that is a natural expression of the gifts and calling of God. Mr. Chambers also wrote, "The call of God is essentially expressive of His nature; service is the outcome of what is fitted to my nature."[2] This is the vocation God has called us to, whether that be in business, in ministry, for the government, as part of a nonprofit organization, or as a parent. It is a place that should stretch us, forcing us to make a daily pull on God's grace to make up the difference between what we can do ourselves and what He is calling us "to reach just beyond our grasp" to accomplish.

"Though it is wonderful to serve because there is a need, there is another level of service that is a natural expression of the gifts and calling of God."

At the same time, true godly service is not something we do alone. Another part of the grace we stir up in helping others is the connections we make with other parts of the body of Christ. As we prosper in our service, we also prosper socially, being energized by doing our part in connection and in concert with others doing theirs. Paul described this dynamic in his letter to the Ephesians:

> *He makes the whole body fit together perfectly. As each part does its own special work, it helps the other parts grow, so that the whole body is healthy and growing and full of love* (Ephesians 4:16 NLT).

Service is taking our place as God's hands and feet on the earth. When we are willing to do that, He will touch our lives in whole new ways.

Prosperity Point

Service offers us not only a chance to fulfill our purpose, but also gives us an opportunity to draw on the grace of God to empower others. It is through service, expecting nothing in return, that we exemplify the heart of God on the earth.

Prosperity Thought

It's the action, not the fruit of the action, that's important. You have to do the right thing. It may not be in your power, may not be in your time, that there'll be any fruit. But that doesn't mean you stop doing the right thing. You may never know what results come from your action. But if you do nothing, there will be no result.

—Mahatma Gandhi

Day Thirty

JUSTICE

Only when we have come to know Jesus as the Judge will we have adequate answers for the most broken people we encounter each day, people who are crying out for justice yet who do not know the One to whom they can direct their cry.
—Shelley Hundley,
A Cry for Justice

Christianity calls for a revolutionary kind of justice. It calls for a turning over of the oppressed and the oppressor to the court of Heaven. It calls for them to be brought before the One Righteous Judge. And it is a call for us to reach out to those God Himself cries for. We are His emissaries, His ambassadors, His missionaries. We are the bearers of His grace that is to be extended to others. This means standing in the halls of human governments to protect the innocent and seeing that the guilty can hurt no one else; it means delivering the captives, restoring the abused, and, if possible, rehabilitating the abuser. It is a huge endeavor, but God has called each of us to it:

> *It's quite simple: Do what is fair and just to your neighbor, be compassionate and loyal in your love, and don't take yourself too seriously—take God seriously* (Micah 6:8 MSG).

To take God seriously is not to dismiss one person as unworthy of our reaching out with His deliverance. We are His ambassadors, after all; we are the ones called to expand the tent flaps of His Kingdom.

The call for justice is the call for a universalization of the Golden Rule: *"Ask yourself what you want people to do for you, then grab the initiative and do it for them."*[1] It is the call to help "our neighbor" just as the Good Samaritan did.[2] It is to take part in the true religion of standing up with the *"homeless and loveless,"*[3]—*"the least of us,"*[4]—and to be proactive in carrying out the same ministry Jesus announced He came to the earth to perform:

> *The Spirit of the Lord is upon Me, because He has anointed Me to preach the gospel to the poor; He has sent Me to heal the brokenhearted, to proclaim liberty to the captives and recovery of sight to the blind, to set at liberty those who are oppressed; to proclaim the acceptable year of the Lord* (Luke 4:18-19).

We are the ones—in God's name—who should be facilitating healing, who should be coming together to find solutions to poverty, to protecting the disenfranchised, and to bringing God's kind of freedom to the earth. Ours should be the most articulate voices standing up against diseases, such as HIV and malaria, against poverty and tyranny, to free the slaves and transform the slave owners, to deliver the addict and liberate the oppressed, to fight for human dignity, empower the marginalized, end development-smothering corruption, and to speak for the silenced.

"It is through empowerment that we help people to help themselves—and those around them."

It is through empowerment that we help people to help themselves—and those around them. Injustice squelches provision, just as we are told in the book of Proverbs:

> *The fallow ground of the poor would yield much food, but it is swept away through injustice* (Proverbs 13:23 ESV).

In this way, injustice stifles the multiplication power of freedom. Exploitation, captivity, and abuse corrupts the soul's own power to create, problem solve, and enrich. Imagine if the collective power of the downtrodden was turned to be productive for themselves and their families. Would poverty have a chance against the realization of such human potential?

At the same time, we are not all called to the front lines where the severest of these battles are taking place, but I do believe we are called to do more than just send money to support those who are. We can be informed, we can raise awareness, and we can join our voices with those dedicating themselves full time to addressing issues of social justice. And we can pray. Never forget we are the ones who have access to the courts of Heaven. We are the ones who can go *"boldly to the throne of grace, that we may obtain mercy and find grace to help in time of need."*[5] We are the ones who can plumb the depths of the mysteries of God looking for answers. We are the ones who can invite the Kingdom of God into any and every situation.

"Darkness will try to keep us out of God's throne room because that is where the real power for change is."

If anything, it is this one thing the enemy will attack more than anything else. Darkness will try to keep us out of God's throne room because that is where the real power for change is. Not only can we then bring these people and issues before God, but we can also catch God's heart and insights for the pressing concerns at hand. We can revive and fill ourselves with His passion for these problems. When we do, we start becoming part of the change we want to see in the world.

Prosperity Point

Justice isn't just a good idea; justice emanates from the character of God. If it emanates from His character, then, as His children, it should also emanate from ours. While these issues can be incredibly difficult, we cannot afford to be cynical about them, because we follow the God of hope. We must stand with those on the front lines of the big social justice issues of our day, be advocates for what they are doing, and accept our place as those who can bring the Kingdom of Heaven to bear.

Prosperity Thought

I would like to be known as a person who is concerned about freedom and equality and justice and prosperity for all people.
—Rosa Parks

Week Seven

VOCATIONAL PROSPERITY

Don't aim at success. The more you aim at it and make it a target, the more you are going to miss it. For success, like happiness, cannot be pursued; it must ensue, and it only does so as the unintended side effect of one's personal dedication to a cause greater than oneself or as the by-product of one's surrender to a person other than oneself.

—Viktor Frankl,
Man's Search for Meaning

Day Thirty-One

PURPOSE

Therefore do not be ashamed of the testimony of our Lord, nor of me His prisoner, but share with me in the sufferings for the gospel according to the power of God, who has saved us and called us with a holy calling, not according to our works, but according to His own purpose and grace which was given to us in Christ Jesus before time began (2 Timothy 1:8-9).

When God called Jeremiah to be a prophet, He told him:

> *Before I shaped you in the womb, I knew all about you. Before you saw the light of day, I had holy plans for you* (Jeremiah 1:5 MSG).

Just like Jeremiah, every one of us is a piece in the overall puzzle of God's will for the earth. We have been designed, not for a particular task, like a cog in a machine, but for a particular niche in partnership with other human beings and God. Our lives are not predetermined or predestined regarding a particular position, but we do have the power to grow into something marvelous and incredibly fulfilling if we learn to walk in step—in *partnership*—with the Spirit of God. We are not automatons in some great cosmic apparatus; rather, we are participants working in dynamic cooperation with the Kingdom of Heaven—co-laboring with Christ[1] toward a better world.

The one great misunderstanding we make with the concept of "calling" is designating those called to work in "the ministry" with some special kind of holiness, as if they had a heavenly directive different from those called to work in business, government, education, entertainment, or for a nonprofit. Though it is a word that has been used less frequently over time, we used to speak of one's calling as their *vocation*. Today, we think of a vocation strictly as "a job," but it also means "a summons or strong inclination to a particular state or course of action," according to the *Merriam-Webster Dictionary*. There was a sense of divinity about this summons or inclination, as if our vocation was somewhat of a godly melding together of who we are—spirit, soul, and body. It was considered something we followed our hearts to find, something our soulish gifts, desires, temperaments, and talents meshed with, and our physical attributes and abilities seemed made for. To find our vocation was our place of wholeness—whether it be in a skyscraper, a village hut, a workers' tent, a lecture hall, or a cathedral.

We have lost a good bit of this sense of vocation in a society where we increasingly separate the sacred from the secular. The separation of church and state was intended to allow people to pursue God according to the dictates of their own heart, but instead has prohibited them from being their "religious" selves anywhere but in their own homes and churches. Thus prayer, for example—one of the greatest problem-solving techniques since the creation of the earth—is seen as intrusive in the places that need problems solved the most. References to the foundations of scriptural truth must be expunged from our monuments and vocabularies. The more we hear such things, the more we subliminally believe that there is a true distinction between our sacred and secular worlds—as if we were better off with split personalities trying to live our one life.

Don't fall for it!

Who you are as a person needs to be brought into wholeness and integration, not fragmentation or compartmentalization. Our calling from God is one. To accept anything else to be true is to believe that the path to holiness is only for those who take the title of Reverend, while the rest of us must straddle between the kingdoms of the earth and the Kingdom of Heaven effectively sullying ourselves in the world for the sake of supporting the work of God.

No!

The work of God has just as much to do with our marketplace jobs—or should I say, "vocations"—our means of income, fulfillment, and all that makes our societies hum. If we are to have a godly society—Heaven on earth—how can that be accomplished unless we also have godly businesses? Unless we are willing to unleash the creative power of the Spirit to bring the innovations in sustainability and technology that we need to improve our world, where do we think those ideas are going to come from?

> *"We need to embrace that our "vocation" is a big part of our God-given purpose and deliberately release His spiritual wisdom, power, and creativity into everything we do."*

We live in a world today that is asking questions about the stewardship of natural resources and the earth as never before. Wouldn't it be good if we got with the Guy who wrote the owner's manual for the universe to accomplish that?

Now I am not saying the primary objective here is to hold prayer meetings and Bible studies in our businesses in the same way we do in our homes and churches (definitely a good thing, but not necessarily the main thing). What I am saying is we need to invite who we are as spiritual beings into the work we do. We need God's endurance sometimes in the things we are asked to accomplish, His innovation in streamlining processes and eliminating waste, His witty inventions, His focus on improving to human experience as the bottom line, His clever frugality that will help us do more with fewer resources, etc. The truth is, we need God in everything we do, and knowledge that the vocations we feel He has called us to "outside" of the Church are as holy, meaningful, and significant as any full-time-ministry type of calling "within" the Church.

God longs to restore this world to the paradise He created it to be. In fact, we are told that, *"Creation waits with eager longing for the revealing of the sons of God."*[2] In other words, nature itself is waiting for us to become who God created us to be!

We need to embrace that our "vocation" is a big part of our God-given purpose and deliberately release His spiritual wisdom, power, and creativity into everything we do.

Prosperity Point

The purpose God has for us will be our place of greatest fulfillment, and where we as human "beings" are the most integrated and complete. As God told Jeremiah, *"I have it all planned out—plans to take care of you, not abandon you, plans to give you the future you hope for."*[3] Listen to the Spirit of God within you, pursue that which inspires you, develop your talents and giftings, and let God guide you into that place where you will not only find "life more abundant,"[4] but also have the greatest impact in expanding the Kingdom of God.

Prosperity Thought

He who has a why to live for can bear almost any how.
—Friedrich Nietzsche

Day Thirty-Two

DILIGENCE

The plans of the diligent lead surely to advantage, but everyone who is hasty comes surely to poverty (Proverbs 21:5 NASB).

I once heard a famous minister tell a group of young leaders, "I can look at your sock drawer and tell if you are going to be successful or not."

Now that made me think. What did he mean by that? What he was talking about was diligence. He was pointing out how much the little details—the details that don't matter to everyone else—really make the difference between success and failure in fulfilling purpose.

You may have heard the word *diligent* thrown around a bit in the past, and you might know that it is mentioned several times in the book of Proverbs, but have you ever really stopped to contemplate what *diligence* really means? What it looks like? If it can be detected from a well-organized sock drawer, is it possible it might mean something more than you had considered it to mean before?

In speaking about diligence, Solomon gives the following advice:

> *Know your sheep by name; carefully attend to your flocks; (Don't take them for granted; possessions don't last forever, you know.) and then, when the crops are in and the harvest is stored in the barns, you can knit sweaters from lambs' wool,*

> *and sell your goats for a profit; there will be plenty of milk and meat to last your family through the winter* (Proverbs 27:23-27 MSG).

Note the care this shepherd takes in doing his job. He knows every single sheep in his flock by name, indicating that he takes personal care to know each individual sheep. That care will be reflected in how the sheep grow and flourish. It is a small thing, but each small detail attended to multiplies down the line. When the flocks are cared for correctly, they are strong and hardy, giving more wool and reproducing. Then, when the harvest has been gathered and the farm or ranch enters the quieter months of winter, there will be wool to knit into sweaters and extra to sell. The unique attention given to each member of the flock results in exponential blessing, even when the farm is in its least productive period.

Look at what else comes for those who choose to be diligent versus those who settle for "good enough":

> *He who has a slack hand becomes poor, but the hand of the diligent makes rich* (Proverbs 10:4).

Diligence tends toward wealth:

> *The hand of the diligent will rule, but the lazy man will be put to forced labor* (Proverbs 12:24).

Diligence tends toward promotion (and avoids *"forced labor"):*

> *Lazy people want much but get little, but those who work hard will prosper* (Proverbs 13:4 NLT).

Those who apply themselves in any area of life will *prosper*—they will enjoy vigorous and healthy growth in whatever realm of their lives they are diligent. Being diligent in them all, however, will have even greater benefits!

Diligence is not just doing good work, though it does start there. In a lot of ways, diligence tends to look a lot like work that doesn't really need to be done at all—it is going the extra mile to get everything just right. To be diligent is to dot every "i" and cross every "t." It is being thorough, doing things with excellence, and stopping to think of the things no one else has taken the time to consider. It is taking care of relationships while at the same time getting the job done, and not at the expense of one thing over the other. It is to hold customers with a high regard while also cherishing your employees. Once again, it embraces the practice of wholeness rather than lock-step priorities.

Another thing about diligence is that it is viral. As you begin to practice it in one area and reap its rewards, you can't help but pass it on to another. Thus the person diligent at keeping his or her desk tidy and organized, for example, has the tendency to keep a neat and organized sock drawer. When you are diligent in your work, you set a higher standard for everything and everyone around you—the lazy will fight against it—but those who catch hold, will prosper.

> *"Those who apply themselves in any area of life will prosper—they will enjoy vigorous and healthy growth in whatever realm of their lives they are diligent."*

Diligence becomes a habit that creates exponential improvement. The slack hand will fall further and further behind in workload and efficiency because of disorganization and clutter. The diligent, however, will incrementally improve and move ahead—never putting off until tomorrow what can be done today. (It also means knowing when to put down your work so you can start fresh the next day—not spending foolishly in one realm of life just to diminish or steal from another.)

Diligence also leads to continual improvement; finding new ways to stay on task, be more efficient, and produce more in the time allotted. Each incremental improvement has a way of building on the last, creating an accumulative effect that can show results in just a matter of days. If this is done consistently over time, the effects can be enormous.

Prosperity Point

Once you begin to understand the concept of diligence, you will see it all through the Bible: Jesus tells us that if we are asked to go one mile, we should be willing to go two, that the good shepherd will leave the ninety-nine sheep to go and rescue the one, that the faithful wife will scour the house to find a lost coin. God is so diligent, in fact, that He knows the very number of hairs on your head and *"clothes the grass of the field, which today is, and tomorrow is thrown into the oven."*[1] He is a God of diligence, and there is much to be gained from emulating Him in His care and attention to detail.

Prosperity Thought

What we hope ever to do with ease, we must first learn to do with diligence.
—Samuel Johnson

Day Thirty-Three

INVESTMENT

I press on toward the goal to win the prize for which God has called me heavenward in Christ Jesus (Philippians 3:14 NIV).

I told the following story in my book *Heal Your Soul, Heal Our World,* but it is so applicable to this idea that I beg your patience to share it again here. Best-selling author Zig Ziglar often shared it when he was speaking:

> On a stretch of railroad track some men were working hard under the sun. A beautiful private train came by, and a man shouted from inside the train in excitement, "Hey Old Jim! Is that you?"
>
> Old Jim, who was hard at work, looked up and replied, "Hi Joe! That's me alright!"
>
> "Jim, why don't you come in here for a cup of coffee?"
>
> Jim hurried in with joy as the sun was hot and he wanted to get into the air-conditioned cabin of this beautiful train. After about an hour or so, Jim came out with Joe and they hugged as old friends would and parted ways. When the train left, the people around asked Jim, "Hey Old Jim, isn't that Joe Murphy, the president of our railway?"
>
> "Sure he is, we have been friends for twenty years now. In fact, we've known each other since the first day we started together working on the railroad."

> "What?! How is it then that he is now the president of the railway, while you are still working here?"
>
> "The answer is very simple. On the first day that we came to work—I came to work for $3.50 per hour, but Joe Murphy came to work for the railway."

This story is a great example of what it means to *invest* versus what it means to *spend*. Old Jim went to work to earn a living, spending his time to earn a basic wage. Joe, on the other hand, invested his time for the railroad, building a career while chasing his life's purpose. The result? A track record of excellence. A legacy of going above and beyond to serve the bigger vision. A pride in ownership that resulted in the kind of quality performance that paid big dividends—an ROI in the form of recognition, raises, and rapid promotion. It wasn't just a job to him; it was a vocation—it was his calling and purpose to see that the railroad thrived so that it could bless its workers and customers alike. As he was as diligent to see that the railroad prospered as he was to get his daily work done, people recognized he had more to offer than just pounding spikes into anchor rails.

Every one of us has three things in our lives that we can choose to spend, waste, or invest: Our time, our talents, and our treasure. The most important and powerful of these is our time, because each and every one of us has exactly the same amount of it every single day. Just because some people are rich or powerful does not entitle them to more than the same twenty-four hours a day that you and I have; however, those people have invested their time in becoming more skilled so they can accomplish more in that time than the average person. If we invest our time in collecting a wage, then that is all we'll ever get; but if we invest our time in making ourselves more valuable by enhancing our talents—expanding our capacity—little by little, day by day, we will begin to see a return on that investment.

However, work is not the only thing we can invest our time in. Have you ever noticed that what is most valuable in our world is what people spend the most time doing? The more time people have spent watching professional sports over the years, the higher salaries in those sports have become. Television is an incredibly lucrative business—more than radio, right? Why? Because people today spend more time watching TV than listening to their radios. Internet companies are exploding in value today because people are spending more and more time on the Internet, especially since we can now carry it with us in our pockets. Social media is one of the fastest growing and most popular activities today, and even though they don't charge consumers for those services, these companies are worth billions in advertising dollars simply because people spend so much time browsing, liking, commenting, and posting on them.

> *"Every interaction and activity of our day is an opportunity for investment."*

At the same time, there are a clever few who have learned to invest their time in social media and are using it to promote their platforms and businesses (we are doing this ourselves at Trimm International), and guess what? Their companies and product sales are growing by leaps and bounds! Where one group wastes time watching video after video, post after post, or reading blog after blog, others are connecting with new customers and getting their message out. Once again, it is in investing their time, talent, and treasure—and activating their expectations that they will see a return—versus simply spending time, expecting to receive nothing other than being entertained, catching up on news, or learning something they never needed to know.

Every interaction and activity of our day is an opportunity for investment. We can invest in the people we meet, in the things that we do, in the thoughts that we think. Our return could be in the improvement of a relationship, in our ability to do things more efficiently, or in learning new and better ways to see problems so that we can innovate solutions. Remember what Peter Drucker said about the Salvation Army and identified as the key to their success? He understood them to be "venture capitalists." They don't just feed the hungry, clothe the naked, or give shelter to the homeless; they *invest* in people hoping to reignite their passion for their God-given purposes. As they do this, there is a palpable commitment to pursuing excellence—it affects attitudes that become contagious—resulting in legendary returns that have made history.

We must never underestimate the power we possess to invest with passion, commitment, and excellence in the opportunities presented to us each day to make a difference. Certainly it is good to sit back, be entertained, and relax—God did instruct us, after all, to take days of rest—but even that is an investment that should nourish our souls and energize our minds and bodies. In the end, it is all about little attitude shifts that can pay incredible dividends in the long run, if we *invest* ourselves rather than *spend* ourselves—purposefully investing our time, our resources, as well as our energy.

Prosperity Point

God gives every one of us the same number of hours in the day—the value those hours have depends largely on how faithfully we steward our talents. Do we increase them so that our hours are worth more, or do we do the minimum required to get by? Are we frugal with our mental, physical, and financial resources so we have a surplus to invest, or do we live without margin, pushing the envelope when it comes to how we care for ourselves—simply because we lack the emotional intelligence to unplug the phone, close our laptops, or turn off the TV to get the rest we need to be our best each day? Sleep deprivation will keep you from maximizing your potential!

Invest your time and energy wisely. And whatever you choose to invest in, invest your whole heart! Invest with excellence. Investment is a powerful Kingdom principle that multiplies your effect wherever you apply it—so invest with purpose. Take some time to consider how to make conscientious, purposeful investment a regular practice in everything you do.

Prosperity Thought

Sentiment without action is the ruin of the soul.
—Edward Abbey

Day Thirty-Four

GOOD WORK

Take care of yourself, have a good time, and make the most of whatever job you have for as long as God gives you life. And that's about it. That's the human lot. Yes, we should make the most of what God gives, both the bounty and the capacity to enjoy it, accepting what's given and delighting in the work. It's God's gift!
(Ecclesiastes 5:18-19 MSG)

Have you ever considered that good work is a gift from God?

But what exactly is good work? If we think about it correctly, good work is something that will stimulate success in as many of the eight realms of life as possible.

First of all, good work will stimulate your spiritual need to live a life of meaning and doing good. In essence, that means your work should provide something for people that makes their lives better, makes them physically, spiritually, and psychologically healthier, while operating lawfully and ethically. It should be something that challenges you to pursue God more closely in order to answer the opportunities you face every day. It is to see His perfect will manifested in what you do. Your work's mission statement should align with the mission you feel God has called you to pursue.

"Your work's mission statement should align with the mission you feel God has called you to pursue."

It should interest you intellectually and push you to learn and grow and perfect your "craft." It should inspire you to read broadly, investigate new topics and research, and maybe even continue your schooling to get advanced degrees. It should challenge you to think and to make better decisions.

It should be a place that makes you excited to get up and get out of bed every morning. It should motivate you to grow as a person. It should encourage the growth of the fruit of the Spirit in your life, and be a place where you can see how your actions contribute to the overall success of your company. While most jobs are stressful at times, good work should allow you a way to handle that stress rather than run from it. It must be something you have the temperament to do, or are motivated enough by to develop that kind of temperament. In fact, it should be a place where you experience joy.

It should also be a place where you prosper physically. This may be the toughest as, in this information age, we tend to spend a lot of time sitting at desks and staring at screens. However, you should be able to find a way to get the exercise you need to better your energy, attention, and performance at work. You may have to exercise on your own time—right after you get up in the morning or over the lunch hour, for example—but whatever job you have, it should allow room in your daily schedule for exercise and eating healthy meals.

Your job should also provide an environment where you can work well as a team with your colleagues. While your relationships should always be professional, that doesn't mean that there won't be a sense of camaraderie, cooperation, and common goals. There should be open and honest lines of communication where feedback is constructive and expectations are high. Supervisors and team members push each other when the chips are down, to be better people as well as better employees. While friendly competition can be beneficial, you should also support and stand up for each other rather than point fingers and blame-shift. There should always be a sense of shared responsibility whether for mistakes or successes. Mutual respect should be evident to all, as if your team were a family.

Your work should also feed your reputation in your community and broaden your personal influence. You can be instrumental in creating a workplace that is an example to others how to be a good steward of the earth, an industry leader for innovation, and have a reputation as a great place to be employed. It should be known for taking care of its customers and contributing to both its community and society. Your work is also your primary place of service to your community—that doesn't mean you shouldn't volunteer for other organizations, but chances are if you work forty or more hours a week, your work is going to be your place of greatest service to others.

Your work should, quite literally, be your calling—your life's vocation. It should encourage you to be more diligent, invest of yourself, and make you ambitious to do more good for others. It should be much more than just a place where you earn a paycheck. It is your place of ministry to humanity, a place you feel "in the zone" of God's will, and therefore it should be fulfilling and joyful.

> *"There are very few things that give our Father a greater thrill than to see us enjoying the work He created us to do."*

And last, your work is almost always your principal place of financial blessing. It will be the place where you create most of your income, especially in the earlier years of your life. It will be the place where you invest your time, increase your talent, and create more treasure to invest in other ways as well as support the work of God around the world. While God is your true Source, it is primarily through your employment that He usually blesses us financially.

Note here the order I addressed each of the eight realms: spirit, intellect, emotion, body, relationship, reputation, vocation, and money. Most look at their occupation primarily from a financial standpoint—and it is biblical to work to earn money to provide food, clothing, lodging, and transportation for ourselves and our families—but then that is the difference between an occupation and a vocation. When you meld these two into one, not only will you have the money to live well, but you will also have a life worth living.

Have you ever noticed what the reward was for the faithful stewards who managed their boss's resources well in the Parable of the Talents?

> *His lord said to him, "Well done, good and faithful servant; you were faithful over a few things, I will make you ruler over many things. Enter into the joy of your lord"* (Matthew 25:21).

Entering into the joy of our Lord—now that sounds like the result of good work, don't you think?

Prosperity Point

Good, fulfilling, community-serving, innovation-creating, friendship-building, intellectually stimulating, financially rewarding work is a blessing of the Lord. God designed you to be like Him: Creative, eager to make things better, and hungry to bless, among other things. Your work gives you an invaluable opportunity to do that. To feel the thrill and flow of good work put you in sync with how God has created you to be, and allow you to daily step into His perfect will. I think there are very few things that give the Father a greater thrill than to see you enjoying the work He created you to do. In this way, working hard can be one of the highest forms of worshiping God.

Prosperity Thought

Choose a job you love, and you will never have to work a day in your life.

—Confucius

Day Thirty-Five

HOLY AMBITION

Once the soul awakens, the search begins and you can never go back. From then on, you are inflamed with a special longing that will never again let you linger in the lowlands of complacency and partial fulfillment. The eternal makes you urgent. You are loath to let compromise or the threat of danger hold you back from striving toward the summit of fulfillment.

—JOHN O'DONOHUE,

Anam Cara: A Book of Celtic Wisdom

Another attribute we have inherited from our Father is the desire to make tomorrow better than today. It is in our nature to create kingdoms and new worlds—to accomplish great things. When we partner with God in our ambitions and seek the expansion of His Kingdom above all else, we make room for ambition to be sanctified and our world to be changed.

Paul was a man of this kind of ambition. Always zealous for God, in his early years he sought to be among the Jewish religious elite and was willing to do horrendous things in pursuit of his goal. He, as he once said of his Jewish brothers, had

> *a zeal for God, but not according to knowledge. For they being ignorant of God's righteousness, and seeking to establish their own righteousness, have not submitted to the righteousness of God* (Romans 10:2-3).

He felt differently after he was confronted by Jesus on the road to Damascus. He realized he had been wrong, he had been selfish, and his ambitions had been misguided. He had been trying to establish his own righteousness, doing what he thought was right but in truth was absolutely wrong. He had a zeal for God that was corrupted and twisted, and thus he did corrupted and twisted things.

By definition, *ambition* is the "drive for success" that pushes us toward our goals. As a practice or value, ambition has a bit of a bad reputation because it has the tendency to emphasize success in one realm of life and for one limited purpose, making us willing to sacrifice all else to accomplish that one thing. It is what has driven many to sacrifice their families and their health for the sake of a prize that too easily slips away when they realize all it cost them. It turns leaders into tyrants and fuels criminal activity—from cartels selling drugs to syndicates profiting from human trafficking. Selfish ambition doesn't care about ethics, doesn't care about the cost to others, nor does it even care about the cost to self. It blinds in so many different ways, and left unchecked, will inevitably lead to a life of regret, even if the goals pursued are accomplished. Much as Paul must have realized soon after he met Jesus on the road to Damascus, ambition can be a terrible taskmaster, justifying the most horrific of actions in the name of whatever goal we put on the throne of our lives.

> *"When we partner with God in our ambitions, we make room for ambition to be sanctified and our world to be changed."*

Much like money, however, the drive to succeed on its own is not necessarily a bad thing; if it is sanctified and focused on the right things, it can instead be an incredible force for good. It combats complacency and can help resist the urge to compromise with the world's prejudices and injustices. It pushes us not just to be better, but to also be the best we can be in every realm of life. Paul described such holy ambition in his letter to the Philippians:

> *Not that I have already attained, or am already perfected; but I press on, that I may lay hold of that for which Christ Jesus has also laid hold of me. Brethren, I do not count myself to have apprehended; but one thing I do, forgetting those things which are behind and reaching forward to those things which are ahead, I press toward the goal for the prize of the upward call of God in Christ Jesus* (Philippians 3:12-14).

Paul chose to put his past and his failures behind him, although he never forgot them; he used them instead to gain wisdom and fuel his passion to fulfill his call in Christ. At the same time, he never dwelled on them, letting condemnation and past conceits derail the reason for which God had laid hold of him. He didn't focus on the past, but on the prize before him of answering the fullness of the upward call of Christ.

So, after regaining his eyesight in Damascus, he started over. All that he had attained before through his political maneuvering, climbing the "corporate" ladder, and doing whatever it was that he saw would get him ahead the fastest—regardless of the cost—he turned away from. He spent—or I should say, *invested*—the next three years studying the Scriptures and praying in Arabia and then again in Syria, letting God teach him from scratch from the same Scriptures he had studied all of his life. It was his own Kingdom university where he reset his paradigms to align them with God and find a new ambition. As he studied the Word of God with new eyes and prayed, a new goal emerged:

> *"Don't ditch your drive—give it to God so that He can redirect it."*

> *The goal of our instruction is love from a pure heart and a good conscience and a sincere faith* (1 Timothy 1:5 NASB).

Paul had adopted a new holistic approach. Beyond self-promotion and a myopic success in one area, people learn to live according to the love of God from undefiled spirits, quickly obeying the dictates of the Holy Spirit through their consciences, and by the type of faith Jesus Himself lived—untainted by selfish desires or self-justification.

And thus Paul's ambition was reborn. In that, he eventually did more for the spread of the gospel of Christ than he had done trying to squelch it. You can't look at that and say ambition is bad, just that it has to be pointed in the right direction.

Prosperity Point

One of the great lies keeping the Church impotent and ineffective in the world today is that ambition must be suppressed if we are to follow God—but that is not true. Yes, *selfish* ambition must be quelled. Yes, we must learn to unleash ambition on bigger goals than our own personal desires, but that doesn't mean we should muzzle the drive that ambition supplies. Instead, we should replace selfish ambition with a drive for excellence, diligently investing our energy in becoming a more excellent version of ourselves. Take the words of Martin Luther King Jr. to heart:

> If a man is called to be a street sweeper, he should sweep streets even as a Michelangelo painted or Beethoven composed music or Shakespeare wrote poetry. He should sweep streets so well that all the hosts of heaven and earth will pause to say, "Here lived a great street sweeper who did his job well."

Don't ditch your drive—give it to God so that He can redirect it. If you do, only God knows what you can accomplish for Him!

Prosperity Thought

And whatever you do, do it heartily, as to the Lord and not to men, knowing that from the Lord you will receive the reward of the inheritance; for you serve the Lord Christ (Colossians 3:23-24).

Week Eight

FINANCIAL PROSPERITY

God can pour on the blessings in astonishing ways so that you're ready for anything and everything, more than just ready to do what needs to be done (2 Corinthians 9:8 MSG).

Day Thirty-Six

ENOUGH

Not that I speak from want, for I have learned to be content in whatever circumstances I am. I know how to get along with humble means, and I also know how to live in prosperity; in any and every circumstance I have learned the secret of being filled and going hungry, both of having abundance and suffering need. I can do all things through Him who strengthens me (Philippians 4:11-13 NASB).

There are only two relationships we can have with money: Either we will serve it, or it will serve us. As the Roman philosopher Seneca not so subtly put it, "Wealth is the slave of a wise man. The master of a fool."

Every day I meet people—good, faithful, believing, Christian people—who slave after money. They have leveraged their credit to the maximum, mortgaging their future, as well as their children's, in the process. Serving money can look like the model of success, when in fact it comes at the cost of an unaffordable mortgage, car payment, or bank loan. Everything is paid by credit card in the hope that next month's paycheck will make up for this month's expenses. On the other hand, it may look like a burgeoning bank account that could finance a new home, vacation, or orphanage, but fear keeps all expenditures at bay. Whether in lack or abundance, when you're serving money, there is never a sense of peace or contentment. No matter what you have, it's never enough.

On the flip side, there are those like the apostle Paul who can look at what they have—whether they are in lack or in abundance—and be content. To them, money is not a goal, but a tool—a means to an end, and that end is not the accumulation of material possessions. They, instead, live to be a blessing to others. They put money to work to bless others, whether that be in the creation of jobs or to help an ex-convict build a new life, whatever they feel God is calling them to do.

What's the real difference in these two groups? If I could boil it down to one thing, it would be the attitude they have toward money. The first group looks at what they have now and sees only their unpaid bills or the calamities that threaten to take it all away. For the other group, they have learned to look at whatever they have and recognize it is *enough.* Then they figure out how to maximize its effects.

I recognized this in looking at two Scriptures:

> *God is able to make all grace abound toward you, that you, always having all sufficiency in all things, may have an abundance for every good work* (2 Corinthians 9:8).

and

> *Godliness with contentment is great gain* (1 Timothy 6:6).

In studying these, I found that they use the same Greek word, *autarkeia,* that appears only in these two verses in the Bible. In 2 Corinthians it is translated "sufficiency"; in 1 Timothy it is translated "contentment." Now look at how these verses would read if I switched the translations:

> *God is able to make all grace abound toward you, that you, always having all contentment in all things, may have an abundance for every good work,*

and

> *Godliness with sufficiency is great gain.*

When I pondered this, I recognized that there is incredible power in looking upon whatever we have as *sufficient* or *enough,* on being *content* with what we have, because money is far from our only resource.

You see, Paul, in his contentment, never trusted money to get him out of a jam—he trusted God. So if he had a little money, he knew he could make it go further because God was on his side. If he needed to, he could always work making tents, or God could provide through a fish with a gold coin in its mouth. God could give him wisdom to make what he had go further, or He could supernaturally multiply it.[1] He knew that if he looked at what he had and declared that he didn't have enough, he was instead declaring he didn't have faith that God could see him through. He knew, whatever he had, that between God and him, they would have *enough* to meet whatever need he faced, whether it was to eat dinner with the group he was traveling with or to supply for the hungry in a region where there had been a drought.

> *There is incredible power in looking upon whatever we have as sufficient or enough.*

I learned this in my own life at a very young age living with a very prudent and frugal single mother. I was the sixth of seven children and we lived in one of the poorer neighborhoods in Bermuda, but poverty never defined us. Certainly there were days when we ran out of everything, including water, but we always had enough for clothing, food, and school supplies. My mother never let us wallow in sorrow about something we wanted and didn't have. Instead, she inspired us to think like entrepreneurs to provide the "extras" we longed for, whether that meant new shoes or ballet lessons. That helped me develop self-discipline and taught me the rewards of hard work. Despite having everything against us, I graduated from college, left the dispirited streets of poverty, and found my way into to the halls of parliamentary leadership.

In this way, I learned never to be limited by how much money we had, but also never to squander it. I figured out how to make it go further in my hand than anyone else I knew, and also how to make it meet a need, even when it appeared not to be enough. I learned the power of contentment and sufficiency—a lesson that has propelled me to achieve things many never aspire to, even though they had more auspicious beginnings than I did.

"To look at what you have now and declare it is "enough," is to acknowledge the power of the God of increase."

Prosperity Point

To look at what you have now and declare it is "enough," is to acknowledge the power of the God of increase—*Jehovah-Jirah:* "The Lord whose provision shall be seen"—as well as to learn to budget your income, control your spending, and invest in what is important in the long run before what you want today. This allows you to manage your finite resources—money, possessions, and time—as well as your limitless resources—your imagination, ability to work smarter, and entrepreneurial ingenuity—to not only meet your own needs, but create enough to give to others.

Prosperity Thought

Content people don't always have the best of everything, but they always make the best of everything.

—Dave Ramsey

Day Thirty-Seven

TRUSTEESHIP

He who is faithful in what is least is faithful also in much; and he who is unjust in what is least is unjust also in much. Therefore if you have not been faithful in the unrighteous mammon, who will commit to your trust the true riches? And if you have not been faithful in what is another man's, who will give you what is your own? (Luke 16:10-12)

To be a trustee is to manage assets on behalf of another. What they manage must be used to fund various projects, endeavors, or institutions as specified by the true owner of the trust. The older term that is more frequently used in the church is "stewardship." It is a term, though, that has been used so often in different ways that I think it has lost much of its meaning.

> *"Stewardship—or trusteeship—is not only about giving what is due to God, but also about handling whatever is left over, no matter how great or small."*

When we hear about "stewardship" in the Christian world today, it is almost all about giving tithes and offerings. It is about being responsible with our money in order to finance our church and the ministries that have touched our hearts the most—and the incredible blessing of giving and living generously when it comes to the work of God. All of this is very good, but it is also a little myopic—so much so that it has created some significant blind spots in our work to expand the Kingdom of God on the earth.

Stewardship—or trusteeship—is not only about giving what is due to God, but also about handling whatever is left over, no matter how great or small. This point is emphasized in the famous "Fifty-Seven Cents" story that follows:

> A pastor happens to pass by a sobbing little girl near a small church. She has been turned away because it was too crowded. Despite her shabby and unkempt appearance, the pastor took her by the hand and both of them went inside. Luckily the girl found a place to sit in the Sunday school class. Because of her joy, she continued to think about the class throughout the evening.
>
> Two years later, the girl died. Her parents called for the kind-hearted pastor who had befriended her that day. The pastor handled the final arrangements. They discovered a little coin purse in one of her pockets. Inside the purse was fifty-seven cents, along with a note that read, "This is to help build the little church bigger so more children can go to Sunday school." The girl had saved the fifty-seven cents over two years. The pastor carried the note and pocketbook to his pulpit the next Sunday morning and told the story of the girl's devotion and unselfish love.
>
> A newspaper heard the story and published it. A realtor read the story and eventually offered the church a parcel of land worth thousands of dollars. However, when the pastor realized the church could not afford it, he symbolically offered the realtor fifty-seven cents for the land.
>
> Church members made contributions in the memory of this selfless little girl. Within five years, the girl's gift had increased to over $250,000.
>
> If you happen to visit the city of Philadelphia, look up the Temple Baptist Church, which now comfortably seats up to

> 3,300 people—and houses Temple University, the Good Samaritan Hospital, and a Sunday school that accommodates hundreds of children so a child will never be left outside during the Sunday school hour. All are situated on the land purchased by that little girl's donation.
>
> In one of the rooms of the Temple Baptist Church, you can see a grainy picture of the little girl whose fifty-seven cents made such remarkable history. Alongside of it is a portrait of her pastor, Dr. Russell H. Conwell.[1]

Imagine the impact this little girl's fifty-seven cents made on that community. For other people, fifty-seven cents may seem worthless, but to the kind pastor who received it, it was more than everything. From that fifty-seven cents, the community was able to build more facilities for children's Sunday school classes, a hospital, a university, and even a new, larger church—all from a few coins one little girl offered her pastor. The power of giving should not be underestimated, for it is the power to change the world.

All of this can be done if we are wise with the money God has given us—if we can see it is enough, and ask God to multiply it and make it a blessing.

Joseph learned this lesson working in Potiphar's house. He gained Potiphar's trust over the years to the point that Potiphar made Joseph the trustee of all Potiphar owned. Joseph then used that money to take care of Potiphar and his household, all of the slaves who worked there, the animals, the fields, and then multiplied it to further increase Potiphar's influence and estate. He did the same when he went to the prison. He became so good at being a trustee, in fact, he was trusted with more and more until Pharaoh ended up making Joseph the trustee of the entire nation of Egypt. Joseph's influence and prosperity increased because he teamed up with God in everything he did and used God's wisdom to prosper whatever he touched.

What if we did that same thing with every dollar that came under our control—into our "trusteeship"? Many of us would have to do things very differently than what I see being done by most Americans today. This would demand a very different perspective of debt, what we really need or want, and the way we manage God's money. It should also dramatically change our priorities in the way we save, invest, and spend. Remember the wisdom found in Proverbs, *"It is possible to give away and become richer! It is also possible to hold on too tightly and lose everything. Yes, the liberal man shall be rich! By watering others, he waters himself"* (Proverbs 11:24-25 TLB).

Prosperity Point

Every penny that comes into our possession is for the advancement of the Kingdom of Heaven. Some is to give away to others working "full time" to expand God's Kingdom, and the rest is for us to use to finance our own ministries. That might mean we start a business or become social entrepreneurs providing incomes for those we employ. It might mean we learn new ways to budget and invest. It might mean that instead of retirement, we save for the day we can head to the mission field without asking anyone for a dime. We should look again at the life of Joseph and recognize the trusteeship principles he lived by, and see how we can use those principles to bless the world around us.

Prosperity Thought

Here's a scary thought: What if God called you to give beyond your comfort level? Would you be afraid? Would you try to explain it away or dismiss it as impractical? And in the process, would you miss out on a harvest opportunity for which God had explicitly prospered you in the first place?

—Andy Stanley

Day Thirty-Eight

STOREHOUSES

The Lord will command the blessing on you in your storehouses and in all to which you set your hand, and He will bless you in the land which the Lord your God is giving you (Deuteronomy 28:8).

Throughout the Bible, God constantly used everyday examples to illustrate spiritual laws and principles. Unfortunately, for those of us today, we sometimes miss the power of some of those illustrations because we no longer live in the culture God was addressing at the time. The blessings listed in Deuteronomy 28 are often diminished by this. If we look at them in context, however, there is a wealth of insight here about financial prosperity and how to handle the blessings of God. Even in the Gospels, as Jesus spoke to the people about material possessions—*"One's life does not consist in the abundance of the things he possesses"*[1]—the agrarian use of storehouses was key to understanding what He meant.

As outlined in the writings of Moses,[2] the Hebrews farmed and measured what they needed each year in terms of storehouses. These storehouses were where they housed and kept their produce safe until another harvest could be gathered to replenish the previous year's storehouse. According to God's dictates, farmers would plant a field for six years and then rest the land during the seventh to give it a Sabbath—in the same way they worked six days each week and took the seventh off. This cycle required the farmer to have the equivalent of three storehouses.

To make this simpler, let's use one commodity—such as grain—to represent all that the farmer, his family, his workers, and his livestock would need to survive one whole year. He would build one storehouse in order to hold all that he and his estate needed to survive for the year, pulling from it slowly as was necessary. He would sell some to buy provisions in the marketplace, but otherwise, they lived off of what he'd saved.

"Wisdom dictated the Israelites have at least three storehouses—faith and their relationship with God would take care of the rest."

As all farmers know, there are good years and there are bad years. If a farmer only kept one storehouse and his crops failed for any reason from drought to locusts, then he would have nothing to feed and maintain his farm until another crop could be harvested. Worse than that, he would have no seed to plant. So the farmer would have a second storehouse for seed to plant in case of crop failure, and a third reserve storehouse to sustain him while the next crop grew.

In the sixth year, before they were to rest the land for a year, God would cause the land to produce threefold, so that they would have enough in store for the year of rest, enough leftover to plant the following year, and still more to live off while that grain was growing. Storehouses were there to catch the extra blessing of God so that the grain wouldn't be spent all at once and not be available for when it was really needed.

So, you will see that the Israelites were used to living with at least three storehouses of grain at all times. This was the responsible way to live—with *two or three years of income* stored away to cover their needs. To have less was foolhardy; to have more was unnecessary. Two to three years of reserves was all the grain they needed at all times unless there were catastrophic problems, such as multiple years of drought, war, or famine. Wisdom dictated they have at least three storehouses—faith and their relationship to God would take care of the rest.

This tells us that the people whom Jesus spoke to were accustomed to having more than enough at any one time. They were so used to this, in fact, that it was something that was in the background of everything Jesus said about God's provision—He never had to mention it because it was a given. People didn't live hand to mouth unless they were beggars. They didn't spend this month's paycheck to pay for this month's rent, or have to wait until payday to buy groceries because they had nothing in their "checking account" (yes, bank accounts are a form of storehouse).

Also, for them, storehouses set very real limits. There was only so much grain in the storehouse. Once it was empty, there was no more. In that respect, storehouses are very different from bank accounts today. If we need more, we can always borrow—and that is where many of us get into trouble. When we get used to using short-term credit card debt to fill in the gaps from the end of our paychecks to the end of our months, we begin to think of our credit card limits as where we need to stop spending—and for anyone who starts bumping up against those on a regular basis, debt becomes an almost inescapable trap.

> *"God blesses you and everything you set your hands to when you follow His mandates for how to manage your money."*

That is why budgeting is so important. Each budget category is like a storehouse if we keep our budgets correctly. When the money in that category is gone, we stop spending until another check arrives and we have more to put into it. If you follow the advice of money teachers such as Dave Ramsey or Larry Burkett, you will have little "storehouses" for your monthly spending—what they call the "envelope system." This works by labeling envelopes for all of the most important expenses each month—the four walls of your house: 1) rent/mortgage and utilities, 2) food, 3) clothing, and 4) transportation expenses—putting money into them at the beginning of each month or week, and then never spending more on those expenses than are in the envelopes.

At the same time, our budgets should include bigger "storehouses" for things such as an emergency fund, a college fund, a fund for health and car insurance, and a retirement fund for the day we can pay ourselves to do what God wants us to do.[3] The more wisdom you can obtain in this area, the better.

Prosperity Point

When Jesus tells the Parable of the Rich Fool in Luke 12:16-21, the audience He spoke to knew that storehouses were important for survival. They knew they had to save in order to have several months of reserves in case of calamity. At the same time, they knew that whatever they had beyond that amount was more than enough—and could be used to build God's Kingdom and help others.

Today we should have the same mentality of saving so that we have money to live off of and take care of ourselves no matter what we face—but also, because we have determined the size those storehouses need to be, whatever else can be given away or invested in others. As Deuteronomy 28:8 makes clear, God blesses you and everything you set your hands to when you follow His mandates for how to manage your money—or, rather, *His* money.

Prosperity Thought

Abundance isn't God's provision for me to live in luxury. It's His provision for me to help others live. God entrusts me with His money not to build my kingdom on earth, but to build His Kingdom in heaven.

—Randy Alcorn

Day Thirty-Nine

THE JOSEPH PRINCIPLE

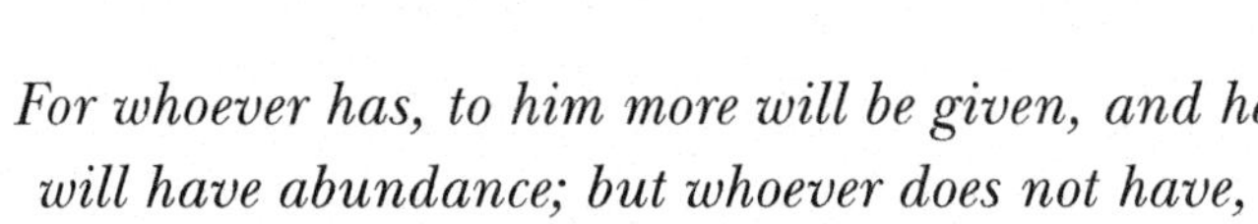

For whoever has, to him more will be given, and he will have abundance; but whoever does not have, even what he has will be taken away from him (Matthew 13:12).

Henry Hartman famously said, "Success always comes when preparation meets opportunity." It is as much about the journey as the destination. Who are you becoming as you journey toward that place of fulfilling God's call on your life? Preparation is a matter of capacity building and character building—both capacity and character are needed to sustain you in any leadership position or place of power. It is about discipline, prophetic foresight, insight, and wisdom. All of these principles can be seen in the life of Joseph.

Remember that day Joseph was brought out of prison to interpret two dreams that were perplexing Pharaoh? They told of a fourteen-year cycle that was coming up—seven years of plenty and then seven years of famine. It is interesting that as soon as Joseph was able to interpret the dream for Pharaoh, he was also able to tell him how to solve the dilemma:

> *Now therefore, let Pharaoh select a discerning and wise man, and set him over the land of Egypt. Let Pharaoh do this, and let him appoint officers over the land, to collect one-fifth of the produce of the land of Egypt in the seven plentiful years. And let them gather all the food of those good years that are*

> *coming, and store up grain under the authority of Pharaoh, and let them keep food in the cities. Then that food shall be as a reserve for the land for the seven years of famine which shall be in the land of Egypt, that the land may not perish during the famine* (Genesis 41:33-36).

Where had Joseph learned this? I believe it is a principle God showed him in managing Potiphar's estate and from how his father had run the family farm back in Canaan. This level of economic and financial savvy does not come from reading textbooks and academic periodicals. It comes from experience. It is simply having managed for seasons using *storehouses*—as we discussed in the last chapter—and recognizing the economic benefits of the laws of supply and demand. At harvest time there will be plenty, and when it comes time to plant again, the farm will produce less. If you don't save the extra during more bountiful months, you will go hungry during months of lack. But what Joseph also learned is that if you have surplus in a season of lack, you can sell it for more at that time than if you sell in a season of plenty. As he applied this principle to Potiphar's estate, it prospered.

In the fourteen-year cycle ahead, Joseph was able to see that what everyone else looked at as a coming disaster, was actually an opportunity. If they could save 20 percent of everything produced by buying it when it was plentiful, they would not only be able to save Egypt from the effects of the famine, but also leverage available resources to build wealth in the process.

The same works in almost every other industry. Take the stock market, for instance. What is the golden rule of making money by trading stocks? "Buy low and sell high." The stock market, as we know, has "bear" markets, when the market is cycling down, and "bull" markets when it is cycling upward. (Of course, knowing when those markets are is much more difficult than figuring out the time of year to plant and the time of year to harvest.) The trick is to basically do the opposite of what everyone else is doing.

When everyone else is selling and driving the price of a stock down, then you wait until it is low enough—ultimately hoping to buy when it bottoms out. Then when everyone else is buying and driving the stock price up, you try to sell at the peak. Not easy to do, of course, but those who save in the bull markets have money to build wealth when bear markets drive prices to "seasonal" lows.

In their landmark book *The Millionaire Next Door,* Thomas Stanley and William Danko reveal it is this very secret that has created wealth for many of America's newest millionaires. When the economy is up and people are spending to benefit from their increased revenue streams, these people are living frugally, but comfortably, saving and only buying what they can get for good deals. They have the emotional intelligence to know that prices will go up when people are buying, so they wait. Then, when the economy is down and prices start to plummet, they begin to buy realizing that prices will eventually go back up, and they can sell when the market is peaking again.

> *"Money itself has no morality, which makes it a heartless dictator if we serve it, but an effective servant if we master it."*

We can see this most evidently in the recent housing bubble. First of all, those who had saved and paid off their homes weren't really affected by the drought of credit that hit so many so hard. Companies that were living hand to mouth, borrowing to pay salaries rather than paying from their own reserves, were suddenly in dire straits. They had to choose between going bankrupt or selling themselves to the highest bidder. Who then bought up those companies? Other companies who had saved when times were good. When many were going into foreclosure on their homes, others were buying up houses for pennies on the dollar compared to what they were once worth. Now, as prices have gone back up, what are those people doing? They are either still renting those properties to maintain a steady income stream, or they are selling those homes for two or three times what they paid for them.

The person who saves when others are spending will then have a surplus to buy at a bargain when others are desperate to sell.

As things turned out for Joseph, at the end of the seven years of famine, the Egyptian government owned everything in the land that could be bought—all of the land, all of the animals, and all of the people! The only thing they didn't own was what belonged to those supported and protected by the government.

In the book of Ecclesiastes, Solomon makes it plain: *"Money answers everything."*[1] It is only those who have a surplus who can give extravagantly; and it is only those who can put money to work for them who will have a surplus. Money itself has no morality, which makes it a heartless dictator if we serve it, but an effective servant if we master it. As best-selling author Ayn Rand said, "Money is only a tool. It will take you wherever you wish, but it will not replace you as the driver."

To master money in this way demands incredible self-discipline, integrity, vision, and patience. It is hard to live frugally when others are living extravagantly. It is hard not to buy on credit instead of saving up—not to buy that new car, house, or whatever else you really want. "Stuffitis," as Dave Ramsey calls it, is a powerful temptation, and one that our economy thrives on. Those selling shoddy, overpriced, aggressively marketed products would not thrive if people had just a little more foresight, emotional intelligence, and more of a "life is a marathon, not a sprint" attitude. As Proverbs 28:20 makes note in The Message:

> *Committed and persistent work pays off; get-rich-quick schemes are ripoffs.*

Every time I read the story of the tortoise and the hare, the tortoise wins. You can argue all you want, but the outcome never changes. The same is true for managing your finances. If you don't know how to save when every aspect of self-indulgence is telling you to buy, you will never be able to build wealth by taking advantage of the Joseph Principle.

Prosperity Point

Those who build wealth recognize:

1. Economies cycle up and down,
2. During times of abundance, they should save the surplus rather than increase their standard of living, and
3. In times of recession, reserves can do double duty by helping others out of a jam, while at the same time building wealth to fulfill the longer-term purposes of God.

As Jesus demonstrated with a little boy's lunch, God multiplies what you have, not what you need. This is why He gives more to those who already have; because He knows He can trust them to do His perfect will with it.

Prosperity Thought

Happiness is not in the mere possession of money; it lies in the joy of achievement, in the thrill of creative effort.

—Franklin D. Roosevelt

Day Forty

LIVING A LIFE OF WORTH

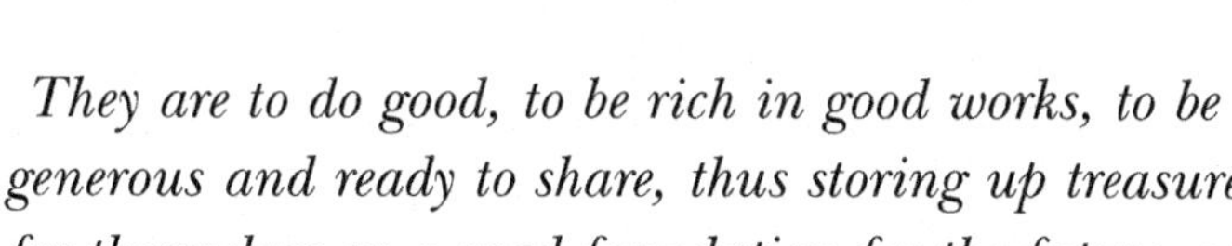

They are to do good, to be rich in good works, to be generous and ready to share, thus storing up treasure for themselves as a good foundation for the future, so that they may take hold of that which is truly life (1 Timothy 6:18-19 ESV).

If you have arrived with me here to this point, having read through the last thirty-nine days, I think you will agree that this has been quite a journey. It is my hope that discussing these prosperity practices has significantly shifted some paradigms for you, offered you a fresh perspective, and given you many new concepts to carefully consider. It is my prayer that this journey has given you tools for constructing a new inner platform of prosperity—providing a springboard for you to begin living a richer, more whole, and integrated life. This is God's ultimate will for you. It is why Jesus came. In John 10:10, He declares, "I have come so that they may have a more abundant life." To quote the New Living Translation, Jesus states here, *"My purpose is to give them a rich and satisfying life."*

On this last day, I also want to explore the words of Paul about what he called, *"the life that is truly life,"* or, as it is in the translation below, *"that which is life indeed."* Take a quick look at the advice Paul gives in the last chapter of his first letter to Timothy:

> *But godliness actually is a means of great gain when accompanied by contentment. For we have brought nothing into the world, so we cannot take anything out of it either. If we have*

> *food and covering, with these we shall be content. But those who want to get rich fall into temptation and a snare and many foolish and harmful desires which plunge men into ruin and destruction. For the love of money is a root of all sorts of evil, and some by longing for it have wandered away from the faith and pierced themselves with many griefs.*
>
> *Instruct those who are rich in this present world not to be conceited or to fix their hope on the uncertainty of riches, but on God, who richly supplies us with all things to enjoy. Instruct them to do good, to be rich in good works, to be generous and ready to share, storing up for themselves the treasure of a good foundation for the future, so that they may take hold of that which is life indeed* (1 Timothy 6:6-10, 17-19 NASB).

In these passages, Paul uses the words *rich* and *riches* in the more common sense of possessions and financial assets. However, you will see he is making the point that if we pursue material goods alone as riches—as so many have unwisely done—it has the potential of drawing us away from God and filling our lives with many sorrows. Money can be an unmerciful tyrant. The only thing that can defeat it is learning to be content with what we have, seeing money as a tool to use to accomplish good things, and choosing true riches—how we positively influence the lives of others—over stockpiling wealth as a tribute to our own greed.

But also look at what he goes on further to say in the next paragraph (1 Timothy 6:17-19). Is Paul calling people rich in worldly wealth evil? By no means! In fact, he expects that Timothy will have rich people in his church (otherwise, how could he instruct them?). Paul advises Timothy to teach the wealthy that their trust should be in God, not their wealth, because He is the true Source of all things enjoyable; that they should invest their wealth—their treasure—in doing good works and being generous, as this will ultimately pay the highest future dividend. Is Paul merely talking about a distant future in Heaven—some future heavenly reward?

No, the context doesn't suggest this. Rather they are building a firm foundation for the rest of their lives, living the type of life that is truly satisfying, truly fulfilling, and the greatest adventure they could ever imagine—the kind of life that is truly living!

Oh, how I long that we could all live that kind of life! But then, that is also the reason we have made this journey! For the key to living a life of worth doesn't come from pursuing the prestige of worldly wealth—but from using the practices of this book to prosper our souls. When we do so, we can't help but become an influence in the places where we live and work. We can't help but minimize the impact of things thrown into our lives to distract us or cause us to stumble—in fact it is possible that those very things could be the stepping-stones that will prosper us most!

"Imagine the type of life you could lead if you continue to grow and thrive in all the realms where God has called you to prosper."

Imagine the type of life you could lead if you continue to grow and thrive in all the realms where God has called you to prosper—to *"abound in all the work of your hand"*[1]—that He might *"set you high above"*[2] and fully establish His Kingdom in your life.

Again, think of God's will for you that Jesus made so clear: *"I have come that* [you] *may have life, and that* [you] *may have it more abundantly."*[3] I firmly believe that kind of life only comes from prospering your soul. It is not a life that comes from merely trying to get by—or by "getting" at all—it has to come from engaging your spirit and prospering in every realm, so you can use that prosperity to prosper others. As Nelson Mandela said, "What counts in life is not the mere fact that we have lived. It is the difference we have made in the lives of others that will determine the significance of the life we lead."

Live so that others may see the Christ in you—these great riches of the hidden truth to be made known—for it is your only hope of glory.[4]

It is my prayer that you can plug into this hope—this glory that comes from within you—a true prosperity that manifests spiritually, intellectually, emotionally, physically, relationally, socially, vocationally, and financially. Remember, it is for you *"God willed to make known what are the riches of the glory of this mystery"* (Colossians 1:27). You hold the keys to prosperity—you are in possession of all that is required to live a rich, fulfilling, enjoyable, abundant, and prosperous life. Oh that you might prosper and be in health even as your soul prospers![5]

Prosperity Point

God is up to something great and He has you in mind. He is not calling you to this kind of prosperous life in order to bog you down with a bunch of unnecessary tasks and demands; He is trying to get you into the abundant life Jesus promised you would have if you followed Him as Lord. It is the life that is truly worth living, and the type of life that will make a difference. As we finish this final day, we have discussed the most important practice for activating true prosperity in your life; tapping into the Christ—the glory—you carry within your own soul.

Here's to a life of prosperity. I pray that you will truly prosper and live a life of extraordinary worth. Live for God. Serve humanity. Make a difference. Change the world. It's your life—make it epic! It's the only life worth living!

Prosperity Thought

The adventure of life is to learn.
The purpose of life is to grow.
The nature of life is to change.
The challenge of life is to overcome.
The essence of life is to care.
The opportunity of life is to serve.

The secret of life is to dare.
The spice of life is to befriend.
The beauty of life is to give.
—William Arthur Ward

If they listen and obey him...they will be blessed
with prosperity throughout their lives
(Job 36:11 TLB).

ENDNOTES

Epigraph

1. 3 John 2.

Preface

1. See Genesis 30:37-39.
2. See 1 John 3:2.
3. See 2 Corinthians 3:18.
4. Colossians 1:27.
5. See 1 Timothy 1:5.
6. See Jeremiah 29:11 NIV.
7. See Hebrews 6:19.
8. See Nehemiah 8:10 and Isaiah 12:3.
9. See Philippians 3:14.
10. *Merriam-Webster Collegiate Dictionary* (Springfield, MA: Merriam-Webster, Inc., 2003), s.v. "prosperous."
11. Ibid., s.v., "prosper."

Introduction

1. See 1 Corinthians 13:13.
2. See Luke 12:13-21.
3 1 Timothy 4:8.
4 See Genesis 39:2-5.
5 See Romans 8:28.
6 See Psalm 34:1.
7. Deuteronomy 8:18 CEB.
8. 2 Corinthians 9:8.
9. 1 Corinthians 15:10.
10. Philippians 4:12.
11. Mark 8:36.
12. Proverbs 4:23 NLT.

Chapter One

1. Ephesians 4:13 NASB.
2. See 3 John 1:2.
3. Romans 14:17.

Chapter Two

1. Proverbs 4:23 CEV.

Chapter Three

1. Luke 16:8.
2. Luke 16:8.
3. Luke 15:2.

Chapter Four

1. Robert A. Watson and Ben Brown, *Leadership Secrets of the Salvation Army* (New York: Crown Business, 2001), Kindle Edition, Loc 513.
2. Matthew 6:10.

Chapter Five

1. Ephesians 2:8.
2. See Hebrews 4:16.

WEEK ONE

Day One

1. Read *Reclaim Your Soul* for more on this topic.
2. Matthew 6:33.
3. Mark 4:19.
4. Mark 4:19.
5. See Hebrews 4:12.
6. 2 Timothy 3:16-17.
7. "Study of the Bible," Sermon Illustrations website, http://www.sermonillustrations.com/a-z/b/bible_study_of.htm (accessed 5/29/14).
8. Psalm 138:2.

Day Two

1. Richard A. Kauffman, "Benedictine Wisdom," *Christianity Today*, December 29, 2008, http://www.christianitytoday.com/ct/2008/december/22.55.html (accessed 5/29/14).
2. 1 Thessalonians 5:17.
3. Romans 12:12.
4. 1 Peter 5:7.

Day Three

1. 1 Timothy 4:12.
2. Proverbs 23:7.

3. "Vilayanur Ramachandran: The Neurons that Shaped Civilization," TED Studies, *Neuroscience—Mapping and Manipulating the Brain,* http://www.wiley.com/WileyCDA/Section/id-816678.html (accessed 6/12/2014).

Day Four

1. For example, the group studies that accompany each of my Soul Series books.
2. See 2 Timothy 2:21.

Day Five

1. Matthew 16:16.
2. Ephesians 3:9.

Week Two

Day Six

1. Anne Kreamer, "The Business Case for Reading Novels," *Harvard Business Review Blog Network* (Jan. 11, 2012), http://blogs.hbr.org/2012/01/the-business-case-for-reading/ (accessed 5/29/14).

Day Seven

1. Colossians 3:23 NASB.
2. David Emerald, *The Power of TED: The Empowerment Dynamic* (Bainbridge Island, WA: Polaris Publishing, 2009), 71.

Day Eight

1. Google Glass, http://www.google.com/glass/start/ (accessed 5/29/14).
2. Mark Bryan with Julia Cameron and Catherine Allen, *The Artist's Way at Work: Twelve Weeks to Creative Freedom* (New York: William Morrow and Company, Inc., 1998), xix.
3. Nick Tart, "How 15 of the world's top brands got started," NBCnews.com, http://www.nbcnews.com/id/40237632/ns/business-world_business/t/how-worlds-top-brands-got-started/#.U0IlRF65fwI (accessed 5/29/14).
4. Natasha Rocca Devine, *Awareness: Creating Your Own Balance in Life* (Bloomington, IN: Balboa Press, 2012), 67.

Day Nine

1. See 2 Kings 13:14-19.
2. 2 Kings 13:19.
3. Mark 4:19 NLT.

Day Ten

1. 1 Kings 3:5.
2. 1 Kings 3:25.
3. 1 Kings 3:26.
4. 1 Kings 3:27.
5. Matthew 6:33.
6. James 1:5.
7. "The History of MADD," MADD, http://www.madd.org/ (accessed 5/29/14).
8. Proverbs 19:8.

Week Three

Day Eleven

1. Galatians 5:22-23.
2. Proverbs 21:15 NASB.
3. Matthew 25:21,23.
4. John 15:11.
5. John 16:24.
6. Romans 14:17.
7. Tommy Newberry, *40 Days to a Joy-Filled Life* (Carol Stream, IL: Tyndale House Publishers, Inc., 2012), 2.
8. Nehemiah 8:10.
9. James 1:4 MSG.

Day Twelve

1. As in 1 John 4:8.
2. Romans 8:6 NASB.

Day Thirteen

1. Martin Luther King Jr., *The Autobiography of Martin Luther King, Jr.,* http://mlk-kpp01.stanford.edu/kingweb/publications/autobiography/chp_19.htm (accessed 6/6/2014).
2. Ibid.

Day Fourteen

1. "Barak Obama's Caucus Speech," *New York Times* website, http://www.nytimes.com/2008/01/03/us/politics/03obama-transcript.html?pagewanted=print&_r=0 (accessed 5/29/14).
2. Ibid.
3. Romans 5:4-5 NLT.

4. Ephesians 1:18 NASB.
5. Hebrews 7:19.
6. Hebrews 3:6.
7. Hebrews 10:23.
8. 1 Peter 1:13 NASB.

Day Fifteen

1. "Angela Lee Duckworth, Psychologist," Ted.com, https://www.ted.com/speakers/angela_lee_duckworth (accessed 5/30/14).
2. See my book *PUSH.*

Week Four

Day Sixteen

1. Galatians 5:22-23.
2. Ecclesiastes 3:11.

Day Seventeen

1. Daniel Goleman, *Emotional Intelligence* (New York: Bantam Books, 1995), xii.
2. Researchers noted that IQ only became a more accurate predictor after the children learned to read.
3. Daniel Goleman, *Emotional Intelligence,* 83.

Day Eighteen

1. Genesis 2:16 NLT.
2. Proverbs 29:18 AMP.

Day Nineteen

1. Genesis 1:10.
2. "Napping," Sleep Resource Center, www.sleepresourcecenter.org/sleep-topics/napping/ (accessed 5/30/14).
3. Louise Atkinson, "Why a rest is as good for you as a sleep (as long as you don't just slob out in front of the TV)," *MailOnline Health,* http://www.dailymail.co.uk/health/article-1313812/Why-rest-good-sleep-long-dont-just-slob-TV.html (accessed 4/30/14).
4. Psalm 46:10 NASB.

Day Twenty

1. Laura Leonard, "Sex and the Single Olympian: Lolo Jones Talks about Her Virginity," *Christianity Today,* August 2012, http://www

.christianitytoday.com/women/2012/august/sex-and-single-olympian-lolo-jones-talks-about-her.html?paging=off (accessed 5/30/14).

2. Psalm 103:12.
3. See 2 Corinthians 7:1.
4. See Matthew 5:8 and 1 Timothy 1:5.
5. Referring to Matthew 5:8.

Week Five

Day Twenty-One

1. Mark 10:51.
2. John 8:11.
3. Note, though, He did hold the disciples to a higher standard, often chastising them with, "*Why are you fearful, O you of little faith?*" when they failed to trust in Him or exercise their faith for themselves. (See Matthew 6:30, 8:26, 14:31.)
4. Luke 17:14.
5. Ibid.

Day Twenty-Two

1. Exodus 21:23-25 NASB.
2. Shelley Hundley, *A Cry for Justice* (Lake Mary, FL: Charisma House, 2011), 150, 155.
3. See Proverbs 18:21.
4. 1 John 1:9.
5. Judith Orloff, M.D., "The Power of Forgiveness: Why Revenge Doesn't Work," *Psychology Today* website, http://www.psychologytoday.com/blog/emotional-freedom/201109/the-power-forgiveness-even-911 (accessed 4/3/2014).
6. Hebrews 12:1.

Day Twenty-Three

1. 2 Samuel 9:1.
2. 2 Samuel 9:7.

Day Twenty-Four

1. Robert Watson and Ben Brown, *Leadership Secrets of the Salvation Army* (Mission Books, 2013), 250.
2. Romans 2:4.

Day Twenty-Five

1. James 3:14,16.

2. James 5:16.

Week Six

Day Twenty-Six

1. Galatians 5:25 NIV.

Day Twenty-Seven

1. Matthew 6:33 NLT.
2. See Matthew 13:31-32.
3. See Matthew 13:33.
4. See Matthew 13:44-46.
5. See Mark 10:23-26.
6. See Matthew 13:47-50.
7. See Matthew 20:1-16 and 22:2-14.
8. Luke 17:21.

Day Twenty-Eight

1. See Mark 4:32.
2. Luke 16:10 NLT.
3. Luke 2:52.
4. Luke 16:12 MSG.

Day Twenty-Nine

1. Oswald Chambers, *My Utmost for His Highest* (Uhrichsville, OH: Barbour Publishing, 1935), January 17.
2. Ibid.

Day Thirty

1. Matthew 7:12 MSG.
2. See Luke 10:29-37.
3. James 1:27 MSG.
4. Matthew 25:40.
5. Hebrews 4:16.

Week Seven

Day Thirty-One

1. 1 Corinthians 3:9.
2. Romans 8:19 ESV.
3. Jeremiah 29:11 MSG.

4. See John 10:10.

Day Thirty-Two

1. Matthew 6:30.

Week Eight

Day Thirty-Six

1. See Matthew 14:13-21.

Day Thirty-Seven

1. Kay McCrary, "57 Cents That Made History," Inspirational Christian Stories and Poems Archive, http://www.inspirationalarchive.com/texts/topics/giving/57cents.shtml (accessed 5/31/14).

Day Thirty-Eight

1. Luke 12:15.
2. See Leviticus 25:1-22.
3. For more information, check out Dave Ramsey's "Seven Baby Steps" and "Financial Peace University" at www.daveramsey.com.

Day Thirty-Nine

1. Ecclesiastes 10:19.

Day Forty

1. Deuteronomy 30:9.
2. Deuteronomy 28:1.
3. John 10:10.
4. See Colossians 1:27 NLT.
5. 3 John 2.

ABOUT DR. CINDY TRIMM

Cindy Trimm has dedicated her life to serving God and humanity. A best-selling author, high-impact speaker, and former senator of Bermuda, Dr. Trimm is a sought-after empowerment specialist, thought leader, and catalyst of cultural change. Listed among *Ebony* magazine's *Power 100* as the "top 100 doers and influencers in the world today," Dr. Trimm is a consultant to civic, nonprofit, and industry leaders around the world. With a background in government, education, psychotherapy, and human development, Dr. Trimm translates powerful spiritual truths into everyday language that empower individuals to transform their lives and their communities. Her message brings new meaning, purpose, dignity, and hope to a global audience.

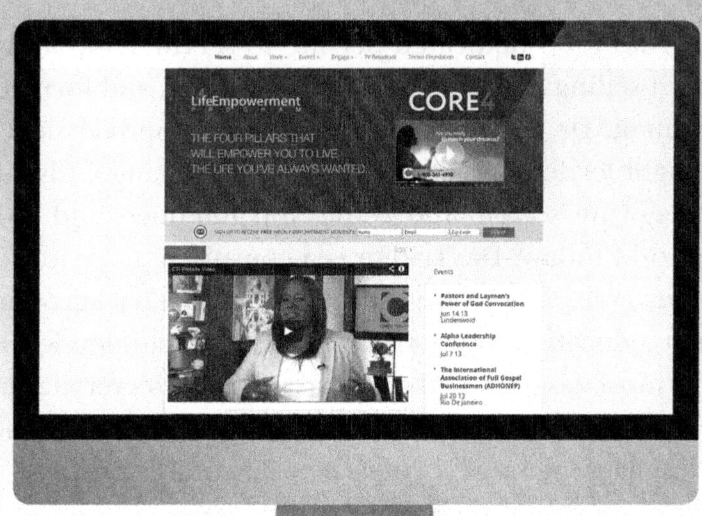

CindyTrimm.com

Let's stay connected!

Be sure to visit us online at *CindyTrimm.com* for lots of online resources to empower, equip and encourage you daily!

Videos • Blogs • Articles

Speaking Event Schedule • TV Broadcast Information

Online Resources • Email Subscribe

...and more!

 @cindytrimm

 facebook.com/drtimm

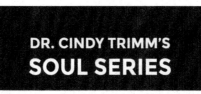

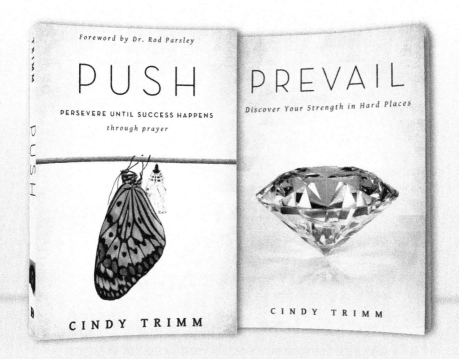

CPSIA information can be obtained
at www.ICGtesting.com
Printed in the USA
LVOW13*0342260118
564089LV00007B/59/P